28
Different
Ways to Pray

The Spirituality Committee

W. Shepherdson Abell

Constance U. Battle

Rev. Lawrence Boadt, CSP

Janice T. Connell

John A. Douglas

Susanne C. DuFour

Anthony Falcone

Lee Leonhardy

Milan C. Miskovsky

James L. Nolan

The Committee acknowledges with appreciation the contributions of Robert P. Holman and Rev. Michael Kerrigan, CSP.

28
Different
Ways to Pray

Written and Edited by Members of the
Spirituality Committee of the
Federal Association, U.S.A.
The Sovereign Military Hospitaller Order of
St. John of Jerusalem, of Rhodes, and of Malta

Paulist Press
New York/Mahwah, NJ

Nihil Obstat:
Rev. Msgr. W. Louis Quinn, P.A.
Censor Deputatus

Imprimatur:
Most Rev. Barry C. Knestout
Auxiliary Bishop of Washington
Archdiocese of Washington
October 20, 2009

The *nihil obstat* and *imprimatur* are official declarations that a book or a pamphlet is considered to be free from doctrinal or moral error. There is no implication that those who have granted the *nihil obstat* and the *imprimatur* agree with the content, opinions, or statements expressed therein.

Cover and book designed by Lynn Else

Library of Congress Cataloging-in-Publication Data

28 different ways to pray / written and edited by Members of the Spirituality Committee of the Federal Association, U.S.A., The Sovereign Military Hospitaller Order of St. John of Jerusalem, of Rhodes, and of Malta.
    p. cm.
    ISBN 978-0-8091-4705-2 (alk. paper)
    1. Prayer—Christianity. I. Federal Association, U.S.A. Spirituality Committee.
II. Knights of Malta. III. Title: Twenty eight different ways to pray.
    BV210.3.A15 2011
    248.3′2—dc22

                                                                    2010025392

Published by Paulist Press
997 Macarthur Boulevard
Mahwah, New Jersey 07430

www.paulistpress.com

Printed and bound in the
United States of America

Table of Contents

Table of Contents

Introduction

For me, prayer is a surge of the heart; it is a simple
look turned toward heaven; it is a cry of recognition and of love, embracing both trial and joy.

St. Thérèse of Lisieux

Prayer has always been at the heart of the Christian life.
There is no single "way to pray." Rather, there are many ways
to pray—the Father's house has many mansions. One of the
great authorities on prayer in the twentieth century was the
English Benedictine Dom John Chapman, who famously
said: *"Pray as you can, not as you can't."*

This little book aims to introduce a variety of prayer
forms, each one being an approach to prayer that many have
found helpful and beneficial to their spiritual life. Whichever form or forms of prayer we settle on, there seem to be
several essential ingredients:

First, we need to devote time to the effort. As Dom
Chapman said:

> The only way to pray is to pray; and the way to pray
> well is to pray much. If one has no time for this, then
> one must at least pray regularly. But the less one prays,
> the worse it goes.

We hear it said that "our work is our prayer," but that
can be a trap. Work—however good—without a base in prayer

can become superficial and rootless. It seems that devoting time explicitly to prayer, on a daily basis, is the best plan. How much time would depend, of course, on our circumstances. Many of us are busy people. Time given to prayer has to come from somewhere. How much can we manage?

Some spend an hour or more a day. For others, squeezing in ten minutes a day seems all that is possible. Experienced spiritual guides counsel that it is better to start modestly and build up gradually, rather than to be over-ambitious—and fail to keep it up. The story is told that, after hearing a rousing talk to a group of priests on the importance of reading Scripture, one priest announced that he was going to begin reading the Bible for an hour a day. The wise man who had given the talk counseled him: "First, just *hold* the Bible in your hand for five minutes a day. When you can do that regularly, come back and we will talk about what comes next."

Most of us need to pray *regularly*. Australian Trappist Fr. Michael Casey, one of today's leading writers on prayer, has noted that our society tends to value spontaneity and flexibility, not regularity. But there is a lot to be said for setting a fixed, regular time to pray. That is because most of us do not look forward to praying and will push it aside for other pursuits if we get half a chance. The discipline of a set time for prayer can help us to actually *do* it, instead of just talking about it. As Fr. Casey says:

> Whether we pray or not depends largely on this willingness to organize our lives....Time is precious and so many things clamor for attention that we will not get around to our spiritual needs unless we arrange a vacant space in which to do nothing else.

Second, we need to choose the right place. Place can be important. Many of us pray at home at least upon rising and going to bed. Jesus told His disciples:

> But when you pray, go to your inner room, close the door, and pray to your Father in secret. (Matt 6:6)

But prayer at work or in a car may also be fruitful. A key is whether the place is one in which we can collect ourselves—and experienced spiritual guides agree that this means *silence*. That is difficult to come by in our hectic lives, yet it is surely essential. How can we be contemplatives in the midst of a busy world? How can this happen without a measure of silence?

Thomas Merton, who had carried on an active life before entering a religious community, certainly found silence among the Trappists. He described its importance:

> Those who love their own noise are impatient of every-thing else....If our life is poured out in useless words we will never hear anything in the depths of our hearts, where Christ lives and speaks in silence. We will never be anything, and in the end, when the time comes for us to declare who and what we are, we shall be found speechless at the moment of the crucial decision; for we shall have said everything and exhausted ourselves in speech before we had anything to say.

Once in the silence, do we find ourselves doing the praying? Or does God do the praying? Paul wrote in Romans 8:26:

> In the same way, the Spirit too comes to the aid of our weakness; for we do not know how to pray as we

3

ought, but the Spirit itself intercedes with inexpressible groanings.

Fr. Casey's view is:

We do not produce prayer. During prayer time we do not attempt to initiate a relationship with God; that relationship already exists. Prayer is an attempt to realize the love that unites us with God, allow it to become more present to us, and give it greater scope to act upon us and to change us. We do not produce prayer. We allow prayer to act.

And as the *Catechism of the Catholic Church* describes it:

God tirelessly calls each person to that mysterious encounter known as prayer. In prayer, the faithful God's initiative of love always comes first; our own first step is always a response. (§2567)

Do we pray for ourselves or for others, or pray simply in adoration? Again, there is no simple answer. Perhaps all three are desirable. Sometimes the prayer of intercession is lost in the enthusiasm for other kinds of prayer. It is difficult to see how we can fail to pray for those others whose lives intersect our own—and for the many whom we never meet, but who are in desperate need.

Prayer itself can lead directly to good works. The Washington, DC, pastor of the nondenominational Church of the Saviour comments:

Our meeting with the person we have prayed for cannot be other than different. That little space in each day when we kneel before God and make intercession does the work of transformation….The veil from my

4

own eyes is lifted. I see that in me which blocks a relationship....We must move toward that day when we do
not have people...who struggle week after week with
the same problem and we are unaware of it because we
are not the kind of people to whom others tell their
problems.

Finally, we need to be realistic about distractions. Of
course, we will meet with distractions. Many experts on
prayer counsel that we cannot really stop distractions from
rushing in—all the things we have to do, faces we have
encountered, memories of events in daily life. What we can
do is to try to keep steadily and calmly on track. Many times
we will look back at our prayer time and wonder how much
focus we really kept. But we should be confident that God
appreciates our making the time for Him—a "burnt offering" of a block of our time, as one writer put it.

Another way of looking at distractions is offered by
Metropolitan Anthony Bloom, the leader of the Orthodox
Church in England:

> Very often people say, "I would like to pray undistract-
> edly, and yet concerns press upon me." Why try to
> push the concerns out? Very often they are God's con-
> cerns, more than ours.

All of these pieces of advice do not add up to a manual
of prayer. Just as there is no single "best" form of prayer, so
also there is no universal way to pray, no one-size-fits-all
structure. We are all different, and we all relate to God
somewhat differently. We each must find our own way.

Further Reading

BOOKS

Bloom, Metropolitan Anthony. *Beginning to Pray*. Paulist Press, 1982. Practical advice from the late leader of the Orthodox Church in England.

Casey, Michael, OCSO. *Toward God*. Triumph Books, 1989, 1996. A profound study of the art of prayer—practical, with deep psychological insights.

Griffin, Emilie. *Doors Into Prayer: An Invitation*. Paraclete Press, 2001. A lovely little series of short and sensible reflections on prayer.

O'Connor, Elizabeth. *Call to Commitment*. The Potter's House Bookservice, 2003. This is a fascinating study of the development of the Church of the Saviour in Washington, DC, with many powerful reflections on the importance of prayer.

COLLECTIONS OF PRAYERS

Kownacki, Mary Lou, OSB, ed. *The Fire of Peace*. Pax Christi, 1992. Prayers focused on peace and justice.

Leach, Michael, and Susan Perry, eds. *A Maryknoll Book of Prayer*. Orbis, 2003. A collection in the Maryknoll tradition.

O'Connor, Cardinal John, et al. *The Catholic Prayer Book*. Servant Books, 1986. A treasury of traditional and new prayers.

Our Family Prayer Book. Ignatius, 2005. An illustrated keepsake prayer book.

Quoist, Michel. *Prayers*. Sheed & Ward, 1999. A series of prayers and meditations that can lead us deeply into reflection.

Introduction

THE *CATECHISM OF THE CATHOLIC CHURCH*

The *Catechism* (available in several editions) is a rich resource for prayer, and itself a starting point for prayer. The entire fourth and final part of the *Catechism* is devoted to this subject.

Prayer: God and Us

> Prayer is the fundamental act of human experi-
> ence, the act that embraces the entire person....To
> pray is to be in the most profound sense possible.
> Karl Rahner, SJ

Have you ever said, "I just need a little peace and quiet"?
Simple rest will help us with fatigue, but what we really long
for is the deeper rest we achieve in prayer. Many people are
leaving the Church for the East to learn prayer and spirituality. They have been taught prayers but not how to pray.
The rush to the East is a symptom of what is lacking in the
West. Most of us are starved for spiritual experience, and
that deep spiritual hunger is not being satisfied in the West.

There was a positive attitude toward contemplation in
the first fifteen centuries of Christianity. The tradition was
that contemplation is the normal evolution of a genuine
spiritual life and therefore open to all Christians. In the six-
teenth century there developed a negative attitude toward
contemplative prayer for the ordinary Christian: it was
believed that contemplation was an extraordinary grace
reserved to the few. Many assumed that contemplative
prayer was reserved for cloistered religious.

There has been renewed attention to contemplative
prayer because of historical and theological studies that
have rediscovered the teachings of St. John of the Cross and
other masters of spiritual life, as well as because of the East's

post–World War II challenge. The idea of laypeople pursuing the spiritual path is not something new. Divine union is the goal of all Christians, and it is the goal of contemplative prayer. It is a mistake to think that a special state of life is needed for doing it. The persons who are most advanced in prayer may be married, may also be engaged in active ministries, or may be running around all day to fulfill their other duties. You only have to be a human being to be eligible to become a contemplative.

As we grow we have what is called a "crisis of limitation" —a period in our lives when we realize our finiteness and our need for God. Possessions do not satisfy us; relationships can disappoint us. There is a dawning sense of neediness that can come over us in regard to God, that He needs to be more a part of our lives. We need to know ourselves as vulnerable and recognize that we cannot go it alone.

Father Armand Nigro, SJ, says that prayer is a personal response to God's presence. Prayer is principally God's work, God's gift. He is present as our Father, loving life into us, sustaining us, and working in us. When we are conscious of God's presence—of God being in and around us—we are in prayer. When we are aware that we move and love in God's loving gaze, we are in prayer. It is noted that the focus is not on *our* efforts but on the activity of God. Our life is prayer. It can be integrated into the unstructured business that marks the way most people spend the time and energy of their lives.

The root of prayer is interior silence. It is the "laying aside of thoughts." It is not so much the absence of thoughts as the detachment from them. Interior silence is one of the most strengthening and affirming of human experiences. There is nothing more affirming, in fact, than the experience of God's presence. That revelation says as nothing else can, "You are a good person. I created you and I love you."

Divine love is compassionate, tender, luminous, and totally self-giving, seeking no reward, unifying everything. The experience of being loved by God enables us to accept our false self as it is, and then to let go of it and journey to our true self. The inward journey to our true self is the way to divine love. The center of gravity of our true self is God. The center of gravity of our false self is itself.

The presence of God is immense, yet so humble; awe-inspiring, yet so gentle; limitless, yet so intimate, tender, and personal: I *know* that I am *known*. Everything in my life is transparent in this presence. It knows everything about me—all my weaknesses, brokenness, sinfulness—and still loves me infinitely. This presence is healing, strengthening, and refreshing. It is nonjudgmental and self-giving. It seeks no reward and is boundless in compassion. It is like coming home to a place I should never have left, to an awareness that was somehow always there, but which I did not recognize. I cannot force this awareness or bring it about. A door opens within me, but from the other side.

There is a growing body of empirical evidence that the emotional traumas from childhood—tension, anxiety, and so on—are stored in the nervous system. In interior silence and the profound rest that contemplative prayer brings to the whole organism, these emotional blocks begin to soften up, allowing the natural capacity of the human organism to throw off things that are harmful start to evacuate them—a kind of divine psychotherapy. The bright light of Divine Love illuminates our innate selfishness.

We all have neurotic tendencies. When you practice contemplative prayer on a regular basis, your natural resources for psychic health begin to revive and you see the false value systems that are damaging your life. The emotional programs of early childhood that are buried in your unconscious begin to emerge into clear and stark answers.

When you truly love yourself, you become aware that your true self is Christ expressing Himself to you, and further: that everybody else enjoys this potential too. Augustine had a phrase for it: "One Christ loving Himself." That is a good description of a mature Christian community. You are aware that a power greater than you is doing everything.

The acceptance of our basic goodness is a quantum leap in the spiritual journey. We have to show compassion to ourselves. We need to befriend our dark side—in truth, not denial—and recognize that God is totally on our side. Our need for healing draws on the infinite mercy and compassion of God. Trust leads to perfect love. When we surrender to God in silence, we begin to heal.

Further Reading

Bloom, Anthony. *Beginning to Pray*. Paulist Press, 1982.

Burrows, Ruth, OCD. *The Essence of Prayer*. Paulist Press, 2006.

Jungmann, Josef A., SJ. *Christian Prayer Through the Centuries*. Paulist Press, 2008.

1

The Mass as Prayer

Nature of the Mass

The Mass is both a series of prayers and a prayer itself. It itself is the most sublime of prayers, and prayer flows out of the Mass. The Vatican II Constitution on the Sacred Liturgy (*Sacrosanctum Concilium*, 1963) opened with a beautiful discussion of the Church as:

> zealous in action and dedicated to contemplation, present in the world, but as a pilgrim....The liturgy daily builds up those who are in the Church, making of them a holy temple of the Lord, a dwelling-place for God in the Spirit. (§2)

That document concluded that the Mass is "the summit toward which the activity of the Church is directed"(§10).

There was a time when Catholics would kneel or sit in the pews and conduct their own private devotions during Mass. This tended to be especially true before Vatican II, when Mass was celebrated exclusively in Latin. Many attended the Latin Mass with great devotion (and still do), but for many others, it was not difficult to disengage from what was actually being enacted at the altar, and concentrate on one's Rosary, or spiritual reading, or private prayers.

Prayerful attention to the elements of the Mass can itself constitute a powerful prayer, and also provide the basis for other prayer during that day or week. The Mass is the formal, communal worship of the Church. The word *liturgy* derives from the Greek word for "public service" or "work," and so liturgy is the "work of the people." We are expected to join in.

The Parts of the Mass

Perhaps we can best cover the subject by moving briefly through the preparation for Mass,[1] the Mass itself, and reflection after Mass. Many Catholics will take a minute or two to prepare themselves for the Eucharistic celebration. One of the great teachers of prayer, Metropolitan Anthony Bloom, the former head of the Orthodox Church in England, suggested something like the following before the Eucharistic Liturgy:

> Lord, I'm going to attend the Liturgy; I'm going to the place which is dedicated to You. It's Your home. I'm going to meet a number of people who love you probably better than I do, who know how to pray better than I pray. What wonder, what a joy, what a privilege. Bless me to go and be wholeheartedly there with You as I would be wholeheartedly at the birthday party of my mother or of my child—as simply and directly.[2]

We remind ourselves that we are praying with (and for) our local community; it is not merely a private connection with God. We join in with the people of our parish, of course, and we should think concretely of them; but we also join in prayer with Catholics around the world. (How many Masses are being celebrated elsewhere at this very moment?)

And the Church wishes that we participate actively, both internally and externally. A moment of reflection can prepare us to do just that.

As the priest enters the sanctuary, most Sunday Masses will begin with an entrance or processional hymn. We should recognize that not all of us enjoy singing in church. Still, it is a real part of the Mass, and we are strongly encouraged to join in. As St. Augustine famously said, "He who sings, prays twice." At weekday Masses (and some Sunday Masses), the congregation may recite the Entrance Antiphon, ordinarily a line or two from the Psalms.

We then pray the penitential prayer (the *Confiteor*, to those of us who recall the Latin from earlier days), "calling to mind our sins." The *Kyrie*—"Lord have mercy, Christ have mercy, Lord have mercy"—again admits our sinfulness three times and begs for mercy each time. The *Gloria*, said on Sundays and at certain other Masses, is a prayer of praise.

The Scripture readings form part of the core of the Eucharistic Liturgy; the Mass is sometimes said to be "the Table of the Word and the Table of the Bread." As Fr. Robert Barron has pointed out, as important as our lived experience is, our faith does not spring from that experience, or from the structures of our psyche, but from revelation. That is what is proclaimed at every Mass.

Another section in this book deals with reading Scripture as a form of prayer; at Mass, the emphasis is on listening attentively to Scripture—itself a form of prayer. But that means that we must listen with an open mind and heart, fully expecting it to have personal meaning for us.

A homily follows the Gospel reading; some homilies, it must be admitted, are more spellbinding than others. But we are asked to listen carefully, and for good reasons. First, as with the Scriptures, listening attentively to the homily can itself be a form of prayer—not unlike reflective spiritual reading. And second, we all share in the priesthood of the laity, and this means that we, too, are obliged to give our own homilies from time to time—not from the pulpit, but when we are called on in daily life to defend the Faith and counsel the doubtful. We need all the help we can get in performing this obligation. Attending to the priest's homily is a good beginning.

We then continue with a series of prayers throughout the Mass. The Creed is a prayer of faith (again, recited on Sundays and certain other times). We move to intercessory prayer with the Prayer of the Faithful, in which we beg God's grace and mercy on members of our community and needy people everywhere. This prayer puts into practice one of the spiritual works of mercy: to pray for the living and the dead. The Offertory Prayer allows us to bring our own gifts, weaknesses, and struggles to the altar.

The Eucharistic Prayer itself is the sum and substance of our faith, and the time for prayer of awe and adoration. The Our Father is the most traditional of our set prayers. Then we offer our own prayers of thanksgiving, during the moments after Communion has been distributed or after Mass.

Our concluding prayers can seem routine—but not if we pay close attention to them. Fr. James Keenan, SJ, tells of a priest in Rome who would always say before the final blessing:

> "You are going to your homes and I to mine; but before I go, I have one more thing to say to you." We paused, savoring the words that he eventually uttered, the words we longed to hear, "The Lord be with you."

The dismissal—"Go in peace to love and serve the Lord"—has been called the most sacred words of the Liturgy after the Consecration. And so the Mass is itself an aggregate of many different kinds of prayer. And yet many of us so often sit through the liturgy without appreciating what a treasury of prayer it really is.

Notes

1. The traditional Tridentine Rite, celebrated in Latin, is also approved for use. The references will be to the much more commonly celebrated Vatican II rite, but some of the points, such as preparation for Mass, will apply to the Tridentine Rite as well.

2. *Practical Prayer* (Conciliar Press, 1989), 16.

Further Reading

The best place to begin is with any good daily or Sunday missal. The monthly publication *Magnificat* contains all the daily Mass readings, morning, evening, and night prayers, and many other helpful features. In addition:

Abell, William S. *The Faithful at Mass.* Georgetown Preparatory School, 1976. Good, but hard to find. Mr. Abell offers a thoughtful and devout guide to participation by the laity in the Liturgy of the Mass (some phrases of which have been borrowed in this chapter).

Barron, Robert. *The Strangest Way: Walking the Christian Path.* Orbis, 2002. A luminous guide to following Jesus in the spiritual life.

Champlin, Joseph. *The Eucharist: A Mystery of Faith.* Paulist Press, 2005.

————. *The Breaking of the Bread: An Updated Handbook for Extraordinary Ministers of Holy Communion.* Paulist Press, 2005.

Dimock, Giles, OP. *101 Questions and Answers on the Eucharist.* Paulist Press, 2006.

Stravinkas, Fr. Peter, MJ. *The Bible and the Mass.* Newman House Press, 2000. Discusses the Biblical roots of the Eucharistic Liturgy.

Fr. Keenan's comments are taken from *The Works of Mercy* (Rowman & Littlefield, 2005).

2

Traditional Prayer

As Jesus taught us by His word and example, daily prayer is essential for all Christians. Our individual prayer life follows the rhythm of our daily life.

Many people think true prayer should be in silence and contemplation, but vocal prayer is an essential part of imitating Our Lord. He taught the apostles to pray the Our Father aloud as their regular prayer, and when in torment in the Garden of Gethsemane, he prayed aloud to his Father. St. Paul tells us that we must pray always (1 Thess 5:17). This does not mean, of course, that we should never stop mumbling prayers under our breath, but it suggests that we need to consecrate the day with prayer, especially prayers of thanksgiving, praise, and petition for God's help—at different times, and on different occasions, and at moments of wonder and recognition of God's presence. This includes praying regularly and often for people who enter our lives. St. Paul again tells Timothy to offer supplication, prayer, petition, and thanksgiving for everyone, including kings and those in authority (1 Tim 2:1–2).

Starting with a morning prayer, we offer our prayers, works, joys, and sufferings of the day to the Lord. During the day, we pray the Rosary with its beautiful familiar prayers: the Sign of the Cross, the Creed, the Our Father, the Glory

Be, the Hail Mary, and the Hail Holy Queen. Before meals, we thank God for our food and often other blessings special to that day. At noon, many pray the Angelus in a prayerful midday pause. Many people adhere to the lovely tradition of praying for a safe journey at the outset of a trip. In the evening, we thank God for everything that happened during the day, and we examine our conscience to make ourselves aware of our thoughts and actions during the day and how well they reflect our desire to be closer to God.

As parents, educators, and grandparents, we teach our children all of the traditional prayers, including special ones, such as the Morning Offering; Acts of Faith, Hope, and Charity; the Prayer to their Guardian Angel; the Act of Contrition; and Morning Prayer and Evening Prayer, which are shorter versions of the Liturgy of the Hours.

A pattern of daily prayer in a consistent manner brings special benefits to us, as St. Thomas Aquinas said so well: "Prayer brings a certain spiritual refreshment of the mind."

In the busy lives we all lead today, it is important to make prayer a part of our day. A quote from St. Augustine from his "Letter to Proba" (*Letter* 130.15):

> Why God should ask us to pray when He knows what we need before we ask Him, may perplex us if we do not realize that Our Lord and God does not want to know what we want (for He cannot fail to know it), but wants us rather to exercise our desire through our prayers, so that we may be able to receive what He is preparing to give us. His gift is very great indeed, but our capacity is too small and limited to receive it.

Further Reading

Davidson, Graeme. *Anyone Can Pray*. Paulist Press, 1983.
O'Collins, Gerald, SJ. *The Lord's Prayer*. Paulist Press, 2007.
Oxford Book of Prayer. Oxford University Press, 2002.
Will, Julianne M., ed. *Catholic Prayer Book for Children*. Our Sunday Visitor, 2004.

Prayer before the Blessed Sacrament

Many Catholics fit in time—frequently, even daily—to "make a visit," to pray in church in the presence of the Blessed Sacrament. Others remain after Mass for a few minutes. Even without entering a church, we can recognize the Lord while passing by one and acknowledge His presence. The founder of the Catholic Worker movement, Dorothy Day, made it a practice to make a visit each day.

Ordinarily, the Eucharist is not exposed on the altar but reserved in the tabernacle. However, frequently a church will arrange for the exposed Eucharist, in a monstrance, to be placed on a main altar or a side altar for veneration and prayer (Eucharistic Adoration, or Exposition). Here, the Blessed Sacrament is removed from the tabernacle by a priest or deacon, who places it in a monstrance (the vessel the church uses to display the Eucharistic Host) and leaves the monstrance on the altar. Sometimes the Exposition will be completed with Benediction. Many parishes have adopted Perpetual Adoration, which is Eucharistic Adoration around the clock, twenty-four hours a day.

The Code of Canon Law provides for churches to be open to permit prayer before the Blessed Sacrament:

Prayer before the Blessed Sacrament

Unless there is a grave reason to the contrary, a church in which the Blessed Sacrament is reserved is to be open to the faithful for at least some hours of every day, so they can pray before the Blessed Sacrament. (c. 937)

Private prayer before the Eucharist has been a long-standing tradition. The practice of Exposition and Eucharistic Adoration is believed to have begun in the year 1226 in Avignon, France. Later in that century, in 1264, the Feast of Corpus Christi was established as a formal attempt by the Church to spread the devotion.

John Paul II wrote in his encyclical *Ecclesia de Eucharistia*:

The Eucharist is a priceless treasure: not only by celebrating it but also by praying before it outside of Mass, we are enabled to make contact with the very wellspring of grace....In many places, *adoration of the Blessed Sacrament* is also an important daily practice and becomes an inexhaustible source of holiness.

And Pope Benedict XVI, when he was Cardinal Ratzinger, wrote in his book *God Is Near Us*:

Only within the breathing space of adoration can the Eucharistic celebration indeed be alive....Communion and Adoration do not stand side by side, or even in opposition, but are indivisibly one.

Mother Teresa, when asked what will save the world, replied:

My answer is prayer. What we need is for every parish to come before Jesus in the Blessed Sacrament in Holy Hours of prayer.

23

Prayer before the Blessed Sacrament is a response to Jesus' request, "Could you not watch one hour with me?" During such prayer, we remain silent, allowing our Lord to draw Himself to us and gently transform us.

There are many ways to pray before the Eucharist. We can actively pray, using traditional prayers; we can remain silent and contemplate the Lord; or we can read Scripture or a spiritual book in the Lord's presence.

Further Reading

Conroy, Susan, ed. *Praying in the Presence of Our Lord with Mother Teresa*. Our Sunday Visitor, 2005.

Groeschel, Benedict J., CFR, ed. *Praying in the Presence of Our Lord: Prayers for Eucharistic Adoration*. Our Sunday Visitor, 1999.

Groeschel, Benedict J., CFR, and James Monti, eds. *Praying in the Presence of the Lord with the Saints*. Our Sunday Visitor, 2001.

Scott, David, ed. *Praying in the Presence of Our Lord with Dorothy Day*. Our Sunday Visitor, 2002.

4

The Holy Rosary

The Holy Rosary of the Blessed Virgin Mary is, as Mother Teresa said, the "spiritual chain that binds generations to eternal life." It is an ancient form of praying with Mary that allows us to walk with her through the mysteries of her Son's life.

The tradition of the Church is that the Rosary was first preached by St. Dominic—founder of the Order of Preachers (Dominicans)—following a vision of the Blessed Virgin. For five centuries, it has been at the heart of the prayer of Catholics individually and in groups (and often around the family dinner table). The Fatima visionaries said that the Virgin stressed the Rosary when she appeared to them.

Where the Holy Rosary has been fervently prayed, reform and renewal have come to families, homes, monasteries, dioceses, parishes, schools, businesses, universities, countries, nations, cities, towns, and villages.

What Is the Rosary?

The Holy Rosary is most frequently prayed by holding a set of rosary beads. A rosary can be made of the most exquisite gems or of the simplest beads (and if a rosary is unavailable, ten fingers can serve as markers for the prayers of the Rosary). As a person says a prayer from the Rosary or meditates upon a scriptural scene, each bead serves as a point of meditation, a reminder to keep one's mind focused on the prayer.

Pope John Paul II was devoted to the Rosary and wrote eloquently about it in his apostolic letter "On the Rosary of the Virgin Mary" (*Rosarium Virginis Mariae*):

> One cannot recite the Rosary without feeling caught up in a clear commitment to advancing peace, especially in the land of Jesus, still so sorely afflicted and so close to the heart of every Christian. (§6)

> After the announcement of the mystery and the proclamation of the word, it is fitting to pause and focus one's attention for a suitable period of time on the mystery concerned, before moving into vocal prayer. A discovery of the importance of silence is one of the secrets of practicing contemplation and meditation. One drawback of a society dominated by technology and the mass media is the fact that silence becomes increasingly difficult to achieve. Just as moments of silence are recommended in the Liturgy, so too in the recitation of the Rosary it is fitting to pause briefly after listening to the word of God, while the mind focuses on the content of a particular mystery. (§31)

In the same letter, he quoted Pope Paul VI:

> By its nature the recitation of the Rosary calls for a quiet rhythm and a lingering pace, helping the individual to meditate on the mysteries of the Lord's life as seen through the eyes of her who was closest to the Lord. In this way the unfathomable riches of these mysteries are disclosed. (§12)

26

The Holy Rosary was from the beginning divided into the Joyful, the Sorrowful, and the Glorious Mysteries of the life of Christ. Each mystery is made up of five decades, and each decade consists of one *Our Father*, ten *Hail Marys*, one *Glory Be to the Father*, and the optional *Fatima Prayer*:

> O my Jesus, forgive us our sins, save us from the fires of hell.
> Lead all souls to Heaven, especially those who have most need of Thy Mercy. Amen.

A fourth group of mysteries, the Mysteries of Light, or Luminous Mysteries, was added by Pope John Paul II in 2002.

Many begin each mystery by meditating on the scriptural scene. After the fifth decade, the Rosary is concluded by praying the Hail, Holy Queen; some follow it with the prayer beginning, "O God, whose only begotten Son…" Both prayers are at the end of this chapter.

If desired, repeat the pattern with the Luminous, Sorrowful, and Glorious Mysteries. Some people thus pray the entire Rosary every day, meaning all twenty decades. Others prefer to pray only one group of Mysteries per day, meaning five decades, which is the design of most rosary beads. Many like to follow this pattern each week:

Sunday: The Glorious Mysteries
Monday: The Joyful Mysteries
Tuesday: The Sorrowful Mysteries
Wednesday: The Glorious Mysteries
Thursday: The Joyful Mysteries
Friday: The Sorrowful Mysteries
Saturday: The Mysteries of Light

Some people pray the Mysteries of Light on Thursdays.

THE JOYFUL MYSTERIES

The first five decades are called the Joyful Mysteries and focus on the joyful scriptural events of the life of Jesus Christ:

The First Joyful Mystery: The Annunciation (Luke 1:26–38). "Then the angel said to her, 'Do not be afraid, Mary, for you have found favor with God. Behold, you will conceive in your womb and bear a son, and you shall name him Jesus'" (vv. 30–31).

The Second Joyful Mystery: The Visitation (Luke 1:39–45). "And Elizabeth, filled with the holy Spirit, cried out in a loud voice and said, 'Most blessed are you among women, and blessed is the fruit of your womb'" (vv. 41–42).

The Third Joyful Mystery: The Nativity (Luke 2:1–7). "She gave birth to her firstborn son. She wrapped him in swaddling clothes and laid him in a manger, because there was no room for them in the inn" (v. 7).

The Fourth Joyful Mystery: The Presentation (Luke 2:22–39). "When the days were completed for their purification according to the law of Moses, they took him up to Jerusalem to present him to the Lord" (v. 22).

The Fifth Joyful Mystery: The Finding of the Child Jesus in the Temple (Luke 2:41–52). "After three days they found him in the temple, sitting in the midst of the teachers, listening to them and asking them questions" (v. 46).

THE MYSTERIES OF LIGHT

These five decades focus on the active ministry of Jesus:

The First Mystery of Light: The Baptism in the Jordan (Matt 3:13). "Then Jesus came from Galilee to John at the Jordan, to be baptized by him."

The Second Mystery of Light: Jesus Changes Water into Wine at Cana (John 2:11). "Jesus did this as the beginning of his signs in Cana in Galilee and so revealed his glory, and his disciples began to believe in him."

The Third Mystery of Light: Jesus Proclaims the Kingdom (Mark 1:14–15). "After John had been arrested, Jesus came to Galilee proclaiming the gospel of God: 'This is the time of fulfillment. The kingdom of God is at hand. Repent, and believe in the gospel.'"

The Fourth Mystery of Light: The Transfiguration (Luke 9:28–29). "He took Peter, John, and James and went up the mountain to pray. While he was praying his face changed in appearance and his clothing became dazzling white."

The Fifth Mystery of Light: The Institution of the Eucharist (Mark 14:22–24). "While they were eating, he took bread, said the blessing, broke it, and gave it to them, and said, 'Take it; this is my body.' Then he took a cup, gave thanks, and gave it to them, and they all drank from it. He said to them, 'This is my blood of the covenant, which will be shed for many.'"

THE SORROWFUL MYSTERIES

The next five decades are called the Sorrowful Mysteries of the Rosary and focus on the sorrowful events of the life of Jesus Christ:

The First Sorrowful Mystery: The Agony in the Garden (Luke 22:39–46; Matt 26:36–46). "His sweat became like drops of blood falling on the ground. When he rose from prayer and returned to his disciples, he found them sleeping" (Luke 22:44–45).

The Second Sorrowful Mystery: The Scourging of Jesus (Luke 23:16; John 19:1). "Then Pilate took Jesus and had him scourged" (John 19:1).

The Third Sorrowful Mystery: The Crowning with Thorns (Mark 15:16, 17; Matt 27:28–29; John 19:5). "They stripped off his clothes and threw a scarlet military cloak about him. Weaving a crown out of thorns, they placed it on his head, and a reed in his right hand" (Matt 27: 28–29).

The Fourth Sorrowful Mystery: The Carrying of the Cross (Luke 23:26; John 19:17; Mark 15:20). "Carrying the cross himself he went out to what is called the Place of the Skull, in Hebrew, Golgotha" (John 19:17).

The Fifth Sorrowful Mystery: The Crucifixion (Luke 23:33–46; John 19:25–30). "Jesus cried out in a loud voice, 'Father, into your hands I commend my spirit'; and when he had said this he breathed his last" (Luke 23:46).

THE GLORIOUS MYSTERIES

The final five decades are the Glorious Mysteries of the Rosary, focused on the power and Glory of the Lord:

The First Glorious Mystery: The Resurrection (Matt 28:2–8; John 20:1–9). "'He is not here, for he has been raised just as he said. Come and see the place where he lay'" (Matt 28:6).

The Second Glorious Mystery: The Ascension (Luke 24:50–51; Acts 1:9; Mark 16:19). "So then the Lord Jesus, after he had spoken to them, was taken up into heaven and took his seat at the right hand of God" (Mark 16:19).

The Third Glorious Mystery: The Descent of the Holy Spirit (Acts 2:1–11). "And they were all filled with the holy Spirit and began to speak in different tongues, as the Spirit enabled them to proclaim" (v. 4).

The Fourth Glorious Mystery: The Assumption (Song 2:10–11; Rev 12:1). "'Arise, my beloved, my beautiful one, and come! / For see, the winter is past, the rains are over and gone'" (Song 2:10–11).

The Fifth Glorious Mystery: The Coronation (Rev 12:1). "A great sign appeared in the sky, a woman clothed with the sun, with the moon under her feet, and on her head a crown of twelve stars."

CONCLUDING PRAYERS

Hail Holy Queen

Hail, Holy Queen, Mother of Mercy, our life, our sweetness, and our hope.

To you do we cry, poor banished children of Eve.

To you do we send up our sighs, mourning, and weeping in this valley of tears.

Turn then, most gracious Advocate, your eyes of mercy toward us

and after this our exile, show unto us the blessed fruit of your womb, Jesus.

O clement! O loving! O sweet Virgin Mary!

Pray for us, O Holy Mother of God.

That we may be made worthy of the promises of Christ.

(Optional)

Leader: Let us pray.

All: O God, whose only begotten Son, by his life, death, and Resurrection, has purchased for us the rewards of eternal life; grant we beseech thee, that meditating on these mysteries of the Most Holy Rosary of the Blessed Virgin Mary, we may imitate what they contain and obtain what they promise through the same Christ our Lord. Amen.

Further Reading

Faley, Roland. *The Mysteries of Light: The Bible and the New Luminous Mysteries.* Paulist Press, 2005.

John Paul II. Apostolic letter "On the Rosary of the Virgin Mary" (*Rosarium Virginis Mariae*). 2002.

Pennington, M. Basil. *20 Mysteries of the Rosary: A Scriptural Journey.* Liguori, 2003.

Reid, David, SSCC. *The Grace of the Rosary.* Paulist Press, 2006.

Also, there are many websites devoted to the Rosary; see, for example, www.familyrosary.org.

5

The Chaplet of the Divine Mercy

Helena Kowalska, later to become Sister Faustina, was born in 1905 in a small village in Poland. She entered the Sisters of Our Lady of Mercy in Warsaw in 1925. She recounted a lengthy series of visions of Jesus beginning in 1931, culminating in the dictation of the Chaplet of the Divine Mercy in 1935. She died in 1938.

In 1993, Pope John Paul II beatified Sister Faustina, and she was canonized in 2000 as St. Maria Faustina. Divine Mercy Sunday is celebrated in many places on the First Sunday after Easter. The pope preached the homily dedicating the Divine Mercy Shrine in 2002, saying:

> How greatly today's world needs God's mercy! In every continent, from the depth of human suffering, a cry for mercy seems to rise up. Where hatred and the thirst for revenge dominate, where war brings suffering and death to the innocent, there the grace of mercy is needed in order to settle human minds and hearts and to bring about peace. Wherever respect for life and human dignity are lacking, there is need of God's merciful love, in whose light we see the inexpressible value of every human being. Mercy is needed in order to

ensure that every injustice in the world will come to an end in the splendor of truth.

Among the visions described by Sister Faustina was one in which Jesus said, "I am offering people a vessel with which they are to keep coming for graces to the fountain of mercy." She also reported other, more specific promises, set out in detail in the publications cited in the bibliography at the end of this chapter. Many people have reported physical and spiritual blessings that they attribute to the Chaplet; again, for details, see the bibliography.

The Chaplet of the Divine Mercy is recited using ordinary rosary beads of five decades. We begin with the Our Father, the Hail Mary, and the Apostle's Creed. Then, on the large bead before each decade, we recite:

Eternal Father,
I offer you the Body and Blood,
Soul and Divinity,
of Your Dearly Beloved Son,
Our Lord, Jesus Christ,
in atonement for our sins
and those of the whole world.

On the ten small beads of each decade, we say:

For the sake of His sorrowful Passion,
have mercy on us and on the whole world.

We conclude by saying:

Holy God,
Holy Mighty One,
Holy Immortal One,

have mercy on us
and on the whole world.

This concluding prayer is to be said three times.

Optional opening and closing prayers, along with a wealth of other information about this prayer, are to be found in the publications cited below.

Further Reading

Diary of Saint Maria Faustina Kowalska. Marian Press, 1987.

Witko, Fr. Andrew. *The Divine Mercy and Sister Faustina.* Catholic Truth Society, 2000.

Also, a number of websites are devoted to the Divine Mercy and contain much detailed information. One such site is www.thedivinemercy.org.

6

Litanies

A litany is a prayer that is made up of a series of invocations or intercessions in the form of a proclamation and a response. Usually a leader recites the invocation and the people respond with a fixed phrase, such as "Amen" or "Pray for us." Litanies are part of the official liturgy of the Church; they can also be used as private devotions. Both the *Kyrie* and *Agnus Dei* of the Mass are litanies, and the Litany of the Saints is part of the liturgies of the Easter Vigil and at ordinations. The solemn prayers of Good Friday are also in litany form. Popular devotional litanies include those of Loreto (to the Blessed Virgin), of St. Joseph, and of the Sacred Heart.

Litanies are prominent in the Bible. In Psalm 136, each verse is a proclamation of God's great deeds, followed by the response, "God's love endures forever." Daniel 3:52–90 is a hymn of praise of God's great acts of creation, each verse followed by "Praise and exalt him above all forever." (Note: In many non-Catholic translations, the litany is omitted from Daniel 3. It is in the text of the Book of Daniel in the New American Bible, which is the standard Catholic translation, or in the widely available New Revised Standard Version with the Apocrypha. There the litany can be found in the Apocrypha under the title the Prayer of Azariah.)

Litanies

In the early Church, the Greek word *litanea* was used for prayers recited while going in procession. Any prayers recited in public processions were included, often prayers of petition for special needs or for forgiveness. In the Western Church, the word gradually became closely linked to the prayer recited by the deacon or cantor in rogation day processions, *te rogamus audi nos* ("We beg you, Lord, hear us!"), to which the people responded, *ora pro nobis* ("Pray for us!"). From this use, the term *litany* came to mean primarily a repetitive prayer and response form.

Rogation Days (April 25 and the three days immediately preceding Ascension Thursday) consist of litanies to God and the saints chanted in procession through a town and the countryside where the priest blessed the land and property. These penitential processions ended at the Church where Mass was celebrated.

The Eastern Church traditions place much emphasis on various litanies within the Eucharist and Divine Office. One of the earliest comes from the *Memoir of Egeria*, a fourth-century pilgrim to Jerusalem. She reported that at Mass the deacon would recite a litany at the dismissal of the catechumens. People would respond, *Kyrie eleison*: "Lord, have mercy!" Private use of litanies is much rarer in the Eastern tradition.

In the West, the *Kyrie Eleison, Christe Eleison, Kyrie Eleison* was used in the fourth century, but not officially required until the sixth century. This period saw the rapid growth of litanies, largely in imitation of Greek Church practice. Most of these centered on petitions for forgiveness, used primarily during Lent. By the seventh century, the Litany of the Saints had developed for processional use, again in imitation of the Greek liturgy. The list of saints varied greatly from place to place until the Council of Trent determined a set form for the whole Church in 1570.

Litanies to individual saints developed later in the Middle Ages. The Litany of Loreto is first known in the twelfth century. Others developed after Trent: the Litany of the Holy Name (approved in 1862), the Litany of the Sacred Heart (approved in 1899), the Litany of St. Joseph (approved in 1909), the Litany of the Most Precious Blood (approved in 1960). Such litanies are popular for local devotions and for Holy Hours because they can be recited without an official minister of the Church presiding, and because the multiplication of honorific titles with the repetition of the responses both intensifies the prayer and makes it more personal and immediate. Litanies are particularly powerful when set to music, and composers see them as ideal for processional hymns.

Litanies are common in the Mass. Some versions of the penitential rite have threefold litanies, as does the *Kyrie eleison* ("Lord, Have Mercy") that follows them. The Prayer of the Faithful is in the form of a litany with a set response, as is the *Agnus Dei* (the "Lamb of God"). Litanies are also encouraged in the sacramental rites. The Litany of the Saints is encouraged in both the sacraments of Baptism and Holy Orders, and there is an intercessory litany in the Mass for the Anointing of the Sick. Ceremonies for religious professions and the dedication of a church, among others, also contain litanies.

A familiar litany is Cardinal Newman's Litany of the Resurrection. It begins with the *Kyrie eleison* and continues:

Christ, hear us. *Christ, graciously hear us.*
God the Father in Heaven, *Have mercy on us.*

God the Son,	
Redeemer of the World,	*Have mercy on us.*
God, the Holy Spirit,	*Have mercy on us.*
Holy Trinity, one God,	*Have mercy on us.*
Jesus, Redeemer of Mankind,	*Have mercy on us.*
Jesus, Conqueror of sin and Satan,	*Have mercy on us.*
Jesus, triumphant over Death,	*Have mercy on us.*

Perhaps the most popular of all litanies is the Litany of Loreto in honor of the Blessed Virgin. Many readers will be familiar with this litany, which recites titles by which Our Lady is known ("Holy Mother of God, Holy Virgin of Virgins," and so on). Such prayers in honor of Mary were known as early as the eighth century, although the current version developed about the year 1200, in association with the Shrine of Loreto, which is claimed to contain the "holy house" of Nazareth in which the Holy Family lived. The litany is particularly powerful because it highlights first Mary's role as mother and virgin, then her fulfillment of titles that come from the Old Testament, and finally her queenship over all. Over the centuries, popes have added at least six new titles to the traditional list. In private use, groups often add new titles that relate to current life, such as "Mother of the Homeless," and more.

As a form of prayer, then, the Litany of Loreto, like all the great litanies, can richly express the link between our ancient faith in what God has done and our contemporary situations and needs.

Further Reading

Martimort, A., ed. *The Church at Prayer: An Introduction to the Liturgy.* Liturgical Press, 1987.

New Catholic Encyclopedia (Second Edition) Volume 8, "Litany," 599–602; "Litany of Loreto," 602–3.

7

Novenas

The word *novena* comes from the Latin word for "nine." It refers to any prayer practice that is repeated nine times. Usually these are performed once a day for nine consecutive days, once a week on the same day for nine consecutive weeks (for example, nine Mondays), or, commonly, once a month (as in remembering a deceased person for nine months, or in observing nine First Fridays or First Saturdays). Novenas can be done in any form, as long as they are done nine times.

The practice of novenas is not part of the official liturgy of the Church, unlike the *octave* (eight days of celebration), which follows major feasts, such as Christmas or Easter. Rather, the novena is part of the private devotions that have been encouraged since the early Church.

The origin of novenas goes back at least as far as pagan Greece and Rome, in which nine days of mourning were observed after a person's death or burial. Early Christians adopted the practice at first, but later changed official mourning to seven days to avoid confusion with pagan practices. But it is still found in the official nine days of mourning for the pope at his death, and in the novena of Masses for the dead that are popular in parishes.

Spiritual writers noted the nine days of waiting that the apostles in the Upper Room kept in prayer between the Ascension and Pentecost (Luke 24:49; Acts 1:4). It became the model for a second purpose of novenas, to celebrate solemn *waiting* in readiness for major feasts. It could take the form of either seeking in prayer special graces from a saint in preparation for his or her feast day, or preparing our hearts devotionally for the major feasts such as Christmas and Pentecost. The first known example of this began in Spain and France in the early Middle Ages with setting aside the nine days before Christmas. This is still observed today with the saying of the special O Antiphons in the Divine Office, beginning December 17 each year.

Novenas can be either public or private devotions. They usually consist of a number of set prayers that are repeated each of the nine occasions. If public, these prayers are recited in common in church. They are often followed by Benediction or connected to Mass, which is then celebrated before or after the prayers are recited. Popular novenas of this type include those to St. Anne, the mother of Mary; to St. Jude, apostle and patron of desperate needs; or to the Blessed Virgin, connected to one of her feasts (such as the popular novena to Our Lady of Lourdes). Public novenas fulfill the promise of Jesus that if two or more people gather to pray for anything whatsoever, God will grant it to them (Matt 18:19). But Jesus also encouraged individual prayer (Luke 11:9–10), and so private novenas can be made at any time and are usually undertaken when praying for a special need or intention.

When praying a novena, it is very important to avoid any sense of superstition or magical power because of the use of nine repetitions. Jesus assured us that all prayer is heard by God (Matt 6:8), and there is no secret power in repeating the prayers nine times. Simply multiplying prayer does not make it more effective in itself (Matt 6:7). On the other hand, nine is a highly symbolic number for Christian tradition, including not only the nine days the apostles waited in prayer, and the image of the nine choirs of angels, but as an imitation of the holy Triduum before Easter, multiplied by three for extra solemnity. Repetition of prayer nine times helps focus our seriousness in prayer, since it requires us to be vigilant and persevering, and to remember to complete the succession of times. This is an excellent way to strengthen our fervent intention in prayer and to commit ourselves to continuing in prayer. It gives witness to the command of Paul to pray always (1 Thess 5:17). Some public novenas have received official recognition by the Church, which has granted indulgences to those who perform them.

Further Reading

Cassidy, Norma. *Favorite Novenas and Prayers*. Paulist Press, 1990.
New Catholic Encyclopedia, second edition, vol. 10, 466–67.

8

The Stations of the Cross

We adore you, O Christ, and we bless you,
Because by your Holy Cross you have redeemed
the world.

The Heritage

Praying the Stations, or the Way of the Cross, the *Via Crucis*, is an honored, long-standing method of meditating upon Christ's suffering and death. It is a popular devotion in both the Eastern and Western Churches. From the earliest times in Christian history, pilgrims to Jerusalem would follow Christ's footsteps from the site of his condemnation by Pilate to his death on the Cross at Golgotha, walking the Way of Sorrow, the *Via Dolorosa*, and pausing to pray at particular places marked for incidents along the way. During the Crusades, knights and pilgrims would follow Christ's way to Calvary.

In order to make this moving devotion more widely available, Franciscans in the fourteenth and fifteenth centuries promoted the practice of imitating these Jerusalem pilgrims by encouraging people to trace steps from Station to Station, identified by a cross and an image of the incident, which had been mounted on the walls of churches or in other locations. Eventually, the Stations of the Cross became an important form for teaching the faith, as well as the muse for great pieces of art. The practice took hold and grew. Today, it is a rare Catholic church or chapel anywhere in the world where you will not find the Stations. Websites for virtual pilgrimages along the Way of the Cross can be found on the Internet.

During Lent, most parishes have a Stations of the Cross service at least once a week. The visual representations, combined with prayers and meditations, help to deepen the community's understanding of Our Lord's loving sacrifice for us and to prompt those walking the path to lovingly respond to Him.

The most important reason for making the Stations of the Cross, whether alone or in a service with the faith community, is that this is a very powerful way to contemplate, and enter into, the mystery of Christ's gift of Himself to us and for us. Reflection on His Passion in this manner moves from our heads to our hearts through the exercise of our imagination. The practice involves our senses, our experiences, and our emotions. By experiencing the love of Christ in such a tangible way, we are prompted to deep gratitude. Gratitude leads us to the desire to love as we have been loved.

The Way of the Cross is commended in the Vatican's *Directory on Popular Piety and the Liturgy*, approved by Pope John Paul II in December 2001. The *Directory* says:

> The *Via Crucis* is a journey made in the Holy Spirit, that divine fire which burned in the heart of Jesus and brought him to Calvary. This is a journey well esteemed by the Church since it has retained a living memory of the words and gestures of the final earthly days of her Spouse and Lord.

In the *Via Crucis*, various strands of Christian piety coalesce: the idea of life being a journey or pilgrimage; as a passage from earthly exile to our true home in Heaven; the deep desire to be conformed to the Passion of Christ; the demands of following Christ, which imply that His disciples must follow behind the Master, daily carrying their own crosses. (Directory §133)

The Stations

The fourteen traditional Stations, revered wherever Catholics are found, are as follows:

First Station: Jesus is condemned to death
Second Station: Jesus is made to bear His Cross
Third Station: Jesus falls for the first time
Fourth Station: Jesus meets His mother
Fifth Station: Simon of Cyrene helps Jesus carry His Cross
Sixth Station: Veronica wipes the face of Jesus
Seventh Station: Jesus falls the second time
Eighth Station: Jesus speaks to the women of Jerusalem
Ninth Station: Jesus falls the third time
Tenth Station: Jesus is stripped of His garments
Eleventh Station: Jesus is nailed to the Cross
Twelfth Station: Jesus dies on the Cross
Thirteenth Station: Jesus is taken down from the Cross
Fourteenth Station: Jesus is buried in the sepulcher

Today, the Church encourages individuals making the Stations of the Cross to continue beyond the Fourteenth Station to meditate on the Resurrection (the Fifteenth Station), concluding the journey before the tabernacle in faith, hope, and thanksgiving.

Praying the Way of the Cross

This devotion is first and foremost a time of prayer. It is a kind of prayer where we enter into a faith experience with Jesus. We see Jesus—what He experiences and suffers for us. This opens our hearts and leads us to respond in love. The Church and many holy men and women have written guides to accompany us on the pilgrimage. Several guides are listed at the end. They offer prayers and meditations that can help us in our prayer journey. Most suggest the following steps before each station:

1. A traditional prayer on approaching each station:

We adore you, O Christ, and we bless you,
Because by your Holy Cross you have redeemed the world.

2. A simple description of the scene, which may be read; for example:

The Second Station: Jesus Is Made to Bear His Cross

Jesus is made to carry the cross on which he will die. It represents the weight of all our crosses. What he must have felt as he first took it upon his shoulders! With each step he enters more deeply into our human experience. He walks in the path of human misery and suffering, and experiences its crushing weight. [From Stations of the Cross, "Online Ministries" Website at www.creighton. edu/CollaborativeMinistry/stations.html]

3. Time spent silently contemplating the scene. Again, guides are available offering meditations or reflections. For example:

Consider how Jesus, in making this journey with the Cross on His shoulders, thought of us, and for us offered to His Father the death He was about to undergo. [St. Alphonsus Liguori's meditation on the Second Station.]

4. Our response expressed in our own words.
5. Concluding prayer(s):

Have mercy on us, O Lord; have mercy on us.

An Our Father, Hail Mary, and Glory Be

6. A traditional hymn while walking to the next station:

"Stabat Mater" ("At the Cross Her Station Keeping")

The Stations of Pope John Paul II

Pope John Paul II revived the tradition of the Bishop of Rome leading the public in the Way of the Cross on Good Friday. The Stations are located at the Colosseum in Rome. On Good Friday 1991, he celebrated an alternative form of the Stations, with each being taken directly from Sacred Scripture. The Scriptural Stations of the Cross of Pope John Paul II are now authorized for use; see www.usccb.org/nab/stations.shtml. Here they are, with the Gospel passage for each:

First Station: Jesus in the Garden of Gethsemane (Matt 26:35–45)

The Stations of the Cross

Second Station: Jesus, Betrayed by Judas, is Arrested
(Mark 14:43–46)
Third Station: Jesus is Condemned by the Sanhedrin
(Luke 22:66–71)
Fourth Station: Jesus is Denied by Peter
(Matt 26:69–75)
Fifth Station: Jesus is Judged by Pilate
(Mark 15:1–5, 15)
Sixth Station: Jesus is Scourged and Crowned
with Thorns
(John 19:1–3)
Seventh Station: Jesus Bears the Cross
(John 19:16–17)
Eighth Station: Jesus is Helped by Simon of Cyrene
to Carry His Cross
(Mark 15:21)
Ninth Station: Jesus Meets the Women of Jerusalem
(Luke 23:27–31)
Tenth Station: Jesus is Crucified
(Luke 23:33–34)
Eleventh Station: Jesus Promises His Kingdom to
the Good Thief
(Luke 23:39–43)
Twelfth Station: Jesus Speaks to His Mother
and the Disciple
(John 19:25–27)
Thirteenth Station: Jesus Dies on the Cross
(Luke 23:44–46)
Fourteenth Station: Jesus is Placed in the Tomb
(Matt 27:57–60)

A Final Prayer

After the final Station, a prayer, adapted from one composed by St. Alphonsus Liguori, might be said:

> O Jesus Christ, my Lord, with what great love you traveled the painful road which led to your death—and how often have I abandoned you. But now I love you with my whole soul, and because I love you, I am sincerely sorry for having offended you. My Jesus, pardon me, and permit me to accompany you on this journey. You died for the love of me, and it is my wish, O my dearest Redeemer, to be willing to die for love of you. In your love I wish to live, and in your love I wish to die. Amen

Further Reading

BOOKS

Enzler, Clarence. *Everyone's Way of the Cross*. Ave Maria Press, 1991.

Guardini, Romano. *The Way of the Cross of Our Lord and Saviour Jesus Christ*. Scepter Limited, 1959.

John Paul II. *Testimony of the Cross: Meditations and Prayers of His Holiness Pope John Paul II for the Stations of the Cross at the Colosseum, Good Friday 2000*. Liguori Publications, 2002.

McKenna, Megan. *New Stations of the Cross: The Way of the Cross according to Scripture*. Image Books, 2003.

Newman, John Henry. *Meditations and Devotions*. Longmans, Green, 1908.

Nouwen, Henri. *Walk with Jesus: Stations of the Cross*. Orbis, 1990.

Vatican Directory on Popular Piety and the Liturgy—Principles and Guidelines, 2001. Found online at www.vatican.va/ roman_curia/congregations/ccdds/documents/rc_con _ccdds_doc_20020513_vers-direttorio_en.html.

WEBSITES

Creighton University's online Stations of the Cross at http://creighton.edu/CollaborativeMinistry/stations. html.

Meditations on the Stations by the Passionist Fathers at www.cptryon.org/xpipassio/stations/index.html.

A Salesian Way of the Cross at www.catholic.org/prayers/ prayer.php?p=48.

Scriptural Way of the Cross with Meditations by St. Alphonsus Liguori at http://www.fisheaters.com/ stations.html.

"Stabat Mater" at http://campus.udayton.edu/mary/resources /poetry/stbmat.html.

U.S. Bishops' Scriptural Stations as celebrated by Pope John Paul II at www.usccb.org/nab/stations.shtml.

9

The Seven Last Words

What are traditionally called the Seven Last Words are actually the last seven times that Jesus spoke, as recorded in the four Gospels. They are a harmonized, meaning a combined, reading of the crucifixion accounts—what Jesus said while dying on the cross—and are a way to meditate and reflect upon his saving mission.

Traditionally, these have been arranged in the following order:

1. *"Father, forgive them, they know not what they do"* (Luke 23:34).
2. *"I say to you, today you will be with me in Paradise"* (Luke 23:43).
3. *"Woman, behold, your son....Behold, your mother"* (John 19:26-27).
4. *"My God, my God, why have you forsaken me?"* (Matt 27:46, Mark 15:34).
5. *"I thirst"* (John 19:28).
6. *"It is finished"* (John 19:30).
7. *"Father, into your hands I commend my spirit"* (Luke 23:46).

While Jesus would have spoken all these words in Aramaic, the Evangelists subsequently translated them into

Greek when writing their Gospels. And yet *"My God, My God, why have you forsaken me?"* is remembered by both Matthew and Mark in the original Aramaic because *"Eloi, Eloi, lema sabachthani"* is a direct quote of the opening verse from Psalm 22. This sentence is the only one of the seven words that is attested to by two Gospels, whereas the other six are unique to a particular Evangelist. The first, second, and seventh words are taken from the Gospel of Luke, whereas the third, fifth, and sixth are found in the Gospel of John.

It is interesting to note parallel words in Luke's Acts of the Apostles when St. Stephen, the first Christian martyr, was being stoned to death by the angry crowd. Stephen spoke words similar to the seventh and first words of the dying Jesus: "Lord Jesus, receive my spirit" (Acts 7:59) and "Lord, do not hold this sin against them" (Acts 7:60). Luke thus highlights how Christians need to follow the example of the cross and to give witness to the faith by speaking and acting like Jesus.

Historically, the Seven Last Words have been used as the basis for meditations during spiritual conferences, retreats, and Lenten missions. They offer a fine biblically based prayer resource for personal or group meditation during Lent and Holy Week, and especially on Good Friday. Gazing upon the image of the cross or crucifix while reading and reflecting upon the Seven Last Words of the crucified Jesus offers a way to pray, meditate, and recall the meaning and saving mystery that the cross symbolizes (cf. 1 Cor 1:18–25).

These words have been used extensively in settings and compositions of sacred music, most notably *The Seven Last Words of Our Saviour on the Cross* by the composer Franz Josef Hayden, who wrote choral, orchestral, and quartet versions of the same work as a meditation. On Good Friday, many churches have a solemn three-hour service of the Seven Last Words, which includes the reading of the Gospels to recall the context for each word, followed by preaching, music, and prayers.

The number *seven* is significant in the Bible since it is often viewed as the number for perfection or completion. These seven last words of Jesus uttered on the cross may be seen as paralleling the words spoken by God during the seven days of creation, described in the first chapter of the Book of Genesis. The Seven Last Words may thus be seen as symbolizing the new creation that occurs with the passion, death, and resurrection of Jesus and the fulfillment of God's plan for the salvation of the world. (Phil 2:5–11)

10

The Jesus Prayer

Many people find fixed repetitive prayer helpful. (See the sections "Traditional Prayer" and the "Holy Rosary.") One of the simplest and most powerful fixed prayers is the Jesus Prayer, which has been a part of the Christian tradition since at least the fifth century.

The use in the West of the Jesus Prayer, or the Prayer of the Heart, has increased in popularity since the mid-twentieth century. It was introduced to many by the book *The Way of a Pilgrim*, written by an unknown, nineteenth-century Russian peasant and translated into English in 1930. The book tells of his wrestling with the problem of "how to pray without ceasing." While St. Paul instructed the faithful at Thessaloniki and throughout the world to "pray without ceasing" (1 Thess 5:17), the prayer itself can be traced back to fifth-century monastic spirituality.

In modern monastic usage, the prayer has become:

Lord Jesus Christ, Son of (the living) God,
have mercy on me, a sinner.

This is an amalgamation of two Gospel prayers. The first is the plea of the two blind men: "Son of David, have mercy on us" (Matt 11:12); the second is the humble request of the publican: "O God, be merciful to me, a sinner" (Luke 18:13). The substitution of the "Son of God" for the "Son of David" evokes the high priest's interrogation: "I order you to tell us under oath before the living God whether you are the Messiah, the Son of God" (Matt 26:63).

In the correspondence between the Egyptian monastics St. John the Prophet and St. Barsanuphe (AD 396 to 446), there is a beautiful treatment of the spiritual life. The two writers recommend examination of conscience, abandonment of one's own will, spiritual direction, and, finally, the invocation of the name of Jesus. St. John disapproved of direct struggle with temptation as being reserved only for those who are "powerful with God...like St. Michael." However, there is another way. "For us, the weak, we have only to take refuge in the name of Jesus."

There is a meditative method of connecting the recitation of the Jesus Prayer to breathing. In this technique one prays unhurriedly "Lord, Jesus Christ, Son of the living God..." while breathing in, followed by "...have mercy on me, a sinner" while exhaling. This is a practice that has a long tradition, stretching back to St. John Climacus, the sixth-century monk of St. Catherine of Sinai Monastery. In his classic work, *The Ladder of Ascent*, he writes, "May the memory of Jesus be united to your breathing...and to your whole life." Repeating the Jesus Prayer with or without "breathing techniques" is not yoga or simply meditation. The difference is the Christian encounter with the living God, Jesus. The postures, techniques, and external form may be similar, but the content is unique to Christian prayer.

Obviously, for the modern man or woman with a busy life filled with activities, this specifically meditative breathing technique of praying the Jesus Prayer may be impractical or otherwise off-putting. The breathing component of this prayer is not at all necessary. But like the other formal prayers of recitation in our tradition, such as the Hail Mary, the Our Father, and the Glory Be, this prayer can be an opportunity to focus our thoughts, our hopes, and our intentions throughout our daily distractions. It should not be thought of as reserved for mystics but rather as a help to focus our lives on Christ. As Pope John Paul II wrote:

> Sacraments and sacramentals are structured as a series of rites which bring into play all the dimensions of the person. The same applies to non-liturgical prayer. This is confirmed by the fact that, in the East, the most characteristic prayer of Christological meditation, centered on the words "Lord Jesus Christ, Son of God, have mercy on me, a sinner," is traditionally linked to the rhythm of breathing. While this practice favors perseverance in the prayer, it also in some way embodies the desire for Christ to become the breath, the soul and the "all" of one's life. (*Rosarium Virginis Mariae* 27)

Further Reading

Anonymous. *The Way of a Pilgrim* and *the Pilgrim Continues His Way*. Harper, 1991.

Brianchaninov, Ignatius. *On the Prayer of Jesus*, 1865. Translated by Father Lazarus. New Seeds Books, 2006.

Maloney, George A., SJ. *The Jesus Prayer for Modern Pilgrims*. Performance Press, 1988.

Mathewes-Green, Frederica. *The Jesus Prayer: The Ancient Desert Prayer That Tunes the Heart to God*. Paraclete Press, 2009.

Monk of the Eastern Church [Lev Gillet]. *The Prayer of Jesus: Its Genesis, Development, and Practice in the Byzantine-Slavic Religious Tradition*. Desclee Company, 1967.

11

The Liturgy of the Hours as Daily Prayer

What Are the "Hours"?

The early Christians followed the Jewish example of praying at specified hours during the day (the third, sixth, and ninth hours, and midnight). Early official documents of the Church laid down a night service and seven official sets of prayers ("offices"). Vatican II set the number of "canonical hours" at seven.

Why Pray the Liturgy of the Hours?

The Constitution on the Divine Liturgy of Vatican II tells us that praying the Liturgy of the Hours has special status, immediately after the Eucharist in importance, as the public prayer of the Church (§83). As Jesus is our High Priest by His sacrifice on the Cross, He is also our High Priest by bringing with Him our earthly prayer of praise of God's glory and work of salvation when He takes His seat at the right hand of the Father. Because Christ has united all humanity to Himself through His high-priestly sacrifice, He summons us all to join in His eternal divine song of praise. And thus the Church consecrates each day and each period of the day to prayer on behalf of itself and all humanity.

One of the most ancient reasons that are given for praying the Liturgy of the Hours is that it fulfills the command of Jesus: "Ask and it will be given to you; seek and you will find; knock and the door will be opened to you" (Matt 7:7); or His comment on the widow who plagued the judge until he gave judgment for her: "Will not God then secure the rights of his chosen ones who call out to him day and night?" (Luke 18:7); or Paul's command to "pray without ceasing" (1 Thess 5:17). The prayer is constructed so that the whole course of day and night are made holy by the praise of God. Those who participate in the Liturgy of the Hours do not just perform the duty of the Church; they also share in its greatest honor: to join Christ as the Church, His bride, before the divine throne, singing God's praises.

In the Eucharist we celebrate the once-for-all, eternal salvation of God, who has redeemed us through the death and Resurrection of Jesus, and who now remains with us forever through the celebration of the Mass. The Liturgy of the Hours in turn offers the balance to the eternal presence of Christ by sanctifying those very finite moments of time in which we must find the eternal. The Gospels record that Jesus Himself prayed at many different hours of the day (Mark 1:35, 6:46; Luke 5:16), and He was faithful to the public prayer of Judaism (Luke 4:16, 24:30; Matt 14:19, 21:13). The Letter to the Hebrews tells us that, at the end of his life, Jesus offered up prayers for us even on the Cross (Heb 5:7). The Acts of the Apostles shows that the early community of the Church, in imitation of its master, gathered in public prayer at all hours of the day (Acts 3:1, 10:9,

16:25). The people were of one mind and heart among all who believed (Acts 4:32).

The Church today continues that prayer of Christ and the apostles as its duty. Having been baptized into a share in Christ's priesthood, the Church community expresses this through its public prayer as the Body of Christ. The prime model for the Church at prayer is the apostles gathered with Mary, the Mother of Jesus, in the Upper Room at Pentecost. There the Holy Spirit came upon them while they prayed. Thus, we also need to remember that every prayer in the name of the Church is really the Holy Spirit at work in us, as St. Paul tells us in Romans 8:26: "The Spirit itself intercedes with inexpressible groanings." The Spirit allows us to call God "Father" (Rom 8:15; Gal 4:6; 1 Cor 12:3; Eph 5:18–20). We are all called to pray individually, but there is a special role for joining in the public prayer of the Church, for it fulfills Christ's promise that "where two or three are gathered together in my name, there am I in the midst of them" (Matt 18:20).

How to Pray the Liturgy of the Hours

There are many different ways to participate in the Divine Office, as the Liturgy of the Hours is often called. All priests are bound by their promise at ordination to say the Office of the Church daily. Monastic orders are founded on the basis of solemnly celebrating the Liturgy of the Hours in its fullest form. Many religious orders of men and women alike make the Liturgy of the Hours a part of their Constitutions. Laypeople are also encouraged to say the Divine Office by both Vatican II's *Constitution on the Divine Liturgy* and by the *General Instruction on the Liturgy of the Hours*, as well as by the exhortation of many popes. Ideally, laypeople and priest will join together in public prayer in a Church each day, but most priests and laypeople say the Hours on their own, using a book of the Liturgy of the Hours.

One can make a major investment and get the complete four-volume edition of the Hours. It is organized by season throughout the year, beginning with Advent in volume 1. Since one has to move around to different places in the volumes, it often seems very difficult for most people to master. One-volume editions are also available, such as *The Prayer of the Church*, which are significantly less expensive and less difficult to use. But one can find shorter versions, specially designed for laypeople, which allow them to share in the prayer without the full complications that the clergy or monastic orders must observe. Many religious orders also use a shorter Liturgy of the Hours, which is then sometimes referred to as Morning Prayer and Evening Prayer.

Whatever level of book one uses, the general outline for saying the fundamental hours of Morning and Evening Prayer is as follows:

Opening: "O God, come to my assistance; Lord, make haste to help me."
[Other variants are also provided for use]
Hymn: Sung when the Office is said in common.
[Other hymns can be used from collections at the end.]
Cycle of Three Psalms: Each follows the pattern:
Antiphon: Always said before the Psalms, and can be said after as well
[The antiphons vary from season to season and for feast days.]
A Psalm
Psalm Prayer [In the morning after the first and third Psalms;
in the evening, after the first and second Psalms]

Scripture Reading
Response to Reading: A two-part phrase repeated
Gospel Canticle: [In the morning, the Canticle of Zechariah
   in Luke 1:68–79;
   in the evening, the Magnificat in Luke 1:46–55]
Intercessions for the Church
The Lord's Prayer
Closing Prayer
Blessing: "May the Lord bless us, protect us from all evil,
   and bring us to everlasting life."

This is the full form of the Hours. Shorter versions may eliminate one or more Psalms, some of the prayers at the end of the Psalms, or the responses. But no matter whether one prays the full Office or a shorter version of it, the prayer sequence provides a balance of Scripture, the praising of God *with* the Psalms of the Church, prayers *for* the Church, and opportunities for personal prayer.

As a spirituality, there is nothing quite like it. We the Church are the Body of Christ, at the same time united to and directed by our head, Christ himself (Col 1:15–20). So whenever we pray the prayer of the Church, we pray *as* Christ, *in* Christ, *with* Christ, *through* Christ, and *to* Christ, as the great patristic writers of the early Church would say. We could also add that, because we are the Church, we pray this form of prayer *within* the Church, *as* the Church, *with* the Church, and *for* the Church. The Liturgy of the Hours sums up the unity of the Church with Christ.

Further Reading

American Ordo. Monthly publication that gives the readings for the day. Priests of the Sacred Heart, P.O. Box 900, Hales Corner, WI 53130; www.poshusa.org. Form

050813 from the same source provides further information.

Christian Prayer: The Liturgy of the Hours. Four volumes, but a one-volume condensed edition is also available. Both from Catholic Book Publishing, 1999.

Magnificat. Monthly publication that has Morning and Evening Prayer, as well as Mass readings for each day of the month, together with brief reflections on the theme of the day and on lives of the saints. *Magnificat,* P.O. Box 822, Yonkers, NY 10702; www.magnificat. com.

See the article on the "Liturgy of the Hours" at www. wikipedia.com.

See also "The Divine Office" article from the *Catholic Encyclopedia* of 1910, available online at www.newadvent.com.

The daily readings of the Divine Office are available at www.liturgyhours.org.

A full bibliography of books and articles on the Divine Office can be found online at www.acpfamilybookstore.org (a division of ACPress.org).

12

Praying with the Bible

Praying with the Bible is certainly one of the oldest formal ways the Church has used in its prayer life. Reciting the Psalms is a direct method of praying the Bible text itself. It is reported as part of Jewish worship as far back as the Book of Chronicles in the fifth century BC, where the Levites sing the Psalms in praise of God (1 Chr 16:7–36). Jesus himself is reported singing the great Hallel Psalms (113–18) at the end of the Last Supper in Mark 14:26 and Matthew 26:30. Following this example, the saying of the Psalms was widely adopted as the official prayer of the clergy in the fourth century, soon after Constantine freed the Church to organize.

From its beginning, the Scriptures were considered as essential to the Eucharistic Prayer. This followed from the Temple practice of readings, prayer, and reflection at the weekly Sabbath service and, above all, the scriptural readings in the great feast of Passover, which Jesus had celebrated at the Last Supper. Because they prayed the Scriptures so fully in the liturgy, early Church writers quickly expanded their use of the Bible to other areas of personal prayer. Scripture as a source of prayer led to writing spiritual commentaries on the books of the Bible, composing biblical hymns, delivering sermons for reflection based on biblical texts, and encouraging the personal reading of the Bible.

The key to praying with the Bible is that we are praying out of the story of the text. Meditation on the words of the Scriptures and their implications for our lives leads us to discern what God asks of us, and to respond in prayers of praise, repentance, or petition. Since the real power lies in the biblical text that we read, scriptural methods of prayer can take almost any shape that centers on reading and listening to the message of the passage. So, biblical prayer can take the form of reading a small passage a day and simply letting it sink in; or it can be serious study of a passage to find out its original meaning and then its use by the Church in subsequent centuries. Biblical prayer can follow the Ignatian method or the method of *lectio divina* (see the sections on those forms of prayer); or it can be quiet preparation for the Sunday readings at Mass. It can be as active as seeking lessons from each passage we read, or as quiet and contemplative as simply imagining what it would be like to be in the story or scene we are reading.

In the end, the most important element is to open the Bible and begin to read it regularly so that it can become the source of prayer for us. Once we have begun, prayer will certainly follow!

What Translation of the Bible Should I Use?

There are many fine translations of the Bible. An excellent one created specifically for prayerful and reflective reading is the new *Catholic Prayer Bible: Lectio Divina Edition* (Paulist Press, 2010). There is also the "standard" Catholic Bible in the United States, the *New American Bible* (NAB), which was refreshed in 2008 with an entirely new translation of the Old Testament books. There are many other good editions, as well, such as *The Catholic Bible: Personal*

Study Edition (Oxford, 1995), or *The Catholic Study Bible Study Edition for the NAB* (Oxford University Press, 2006 revised). Both have well-done introductions, discussions of the individual books, and the official NAB footnotes. The *New Revised Standard Version* is also an approved Catholic translation, which is readable and yet especially faithful to the original Hebrew and Greek texts. The *Jerusalem Bible* (1966) is a less literal rendering, but often captures a more accurate sense, and the spirit, of ancient texts with a fresh and lively approach. The *New Jerusalem Bible* (1990) is also lively but somewhat less daring than its original edition was.

Further Reading

Magrassi, Mariano, OSB. *Praying the Bible: An Introduction to Lectio Divina*. Liturgical Press, 1998.

Pennington, Basil, OCSO, and Luke Dysinger, OSB. *An Invitation to Centering Prayer, Including an Introduction to Lectio Divina*. Liguori/Triumph, 2001.

13

The Psalms as Personal Prayer

The Psalms have been called "the prayer book of the Church" because of the special emphasis they receive in our Christian life of prayer. First, they are deeply embedded in the official liturgy of the Church. Every reading from the Scriptures at the Eucharist has a selection from the Psalms used as a response that is intended to echo its major theme and turn the reading from mere learning into the prayer of the community. Recitation of the Psalms is also the center of the official daily prayer of the Church, the Divine Office, obligatory for all ordained members to perform as a prayer in the name of the whole Church. Second, the Psalms have long been the most quoted book of the Old Testament by spiritual writers, and have been seen as particularly valuable prayers for understanding the mystery of Christ. All of us have seen small copies of the New Testament bound together with the Psalms for personal use.

So how can we make the best use of the rich treasury of the Psalter in daily prayer? A number of steps can be suggested to begin the process:

1. Put a marker in your Bible at the Psalms so they are easy to find. Even better, perhaps, would be

to buy a separate little book of all the Psalms for easy prayer.

2. Read through all of the Psalms quickly at one sitting, to get a sense of all their different styles and moods, as well as the different lengths.

3. Read the introductory material that is usually given just before the Book of Psalms in your Bible edition and note some simple keys to the different types:

   a. Look at the headings of each Psalm and note which are called "Psalms of David" or are connected to someone else.

   b. See any special notes in the heading about the musical settings or historical events the editors thought this particular Psalm was linked to.

   c. Check and see if there are stanzas or sections to a Psalm and how your editors have divided it in your copy of the Bible.

   d. Check if the Psalm is called a lament, a hymn of praise, a thanksgiving, or something else, and look for that spirit in the Psalm as you read it.

4. Have a highlighter or pen or pencil ready at your side to mark off any and all lines that strike you as especially beautiful or pertinent to you. Put a note in the margin next to a line that strikes you, or next to a prayer line you would like to make your own. Highlight any key words you note recurring in the Psalm, as well as all the adjectives or nouns that pertain to

God's goodness, such as his titles, his actions, his qualities, and so on.

5. Read just a moderate amount each day. If there are many small Psalms in a row, you can do three or four; if it is a long Psalm, read just the one. If you encounter a line that resonates with you, stay with it for a while—even if you read less than one Psalm that day.

6. Check editorial notes at the bottom of the page for better understanding of the Psalm. Better yet, get a small commentary on the Psalms and read the few lines about this particular Psalm you are praying today.

If you take the time to look closely at a Psalm, you will get much more out of it, and the Psalm will last with you much longer. And there are some other things you can do to let the Psalms enrich your life. Have a piece of paper in your Bible to keep a list of Psalms that you like or see as valuable for different special moments (sickness, anniversaries, doubt, blessings, thanksgiving, and more). Try reading the Psalms aloud to yourself—they will be more powerful, and you will see the poetry in them more readily when you hear yourself saying them. Translate the situation of the Psalmist from his ancient world into your life by imagining what this Psalm would mean in your problems and needs today.

Some people find the descriptions of violence and the spirit of vengeance in certain Psalms difficult to handle. Remember that they were written by people long ago and very different from us, who understood God to redress all wrongs in the same way that the evil was done, and who lived in a social world of tribes and nations where all evil was personal and needed to be punished directly and immediately. God was their personal protector so they expected that He would treat outsiders harshly if they harmed His people. The Bible itself moves toward a broader understanding of God's governance of all peoples equally and the need for trust and acceptance of suffering instead of God's intervention by force. This view is clear in passages like Isaiah 2:1–4 and many others, including many of the Psalms, but still the older sense of dependence on God as our protector and righter of wrongs remained strong. We need to accept that this is how they thought even if we don't (and, as we know, we often do think that way ourselves despite our desire not to!).

Many Psalms are laments seeking help in tragedy. They are by nature passionate and express the natural wish for vengeance. It is actually good for us to express such dark feelings because, as we put them into the words of the Psalm, we hand them over into God's hands and feel some relief at having "gotten it off our chest." Amazingly, such violent pleading with God often helps us to accept God's will and let go of our anger or fear. Finally, if, despite what is suggested here, you still have trouble with a particular Psalm, avoid it! There are many others.

One last word about the beauty of the Psalter. As you read, remember that Jesus also said the Psalms and found in them the way to address His Father with the language of the Old Testament covenant promise. Christians have prayed the Psalms all these centuries, not as joining in a Jewish prayer, but as praying the prayer of Christ. Traditionally, the Church embraces our communion with our Jewish brothers and sisters in the praying of the Psalms—but it also goes beyond that to identify the entire spiritual dynamic of the Psalter with Christ Himself. In the words of the patristic writers, when we pray the psalms, we pray *with* Christ, *in* Christ, and *to* Christ; and we also hear Christ speaking to us.

Further Reading

Knight, George A. F. *Psalms* (2 vols.) OT Daily Bible Study Series. Westminster John Knox Press, 2006.

Quillo, Ronald. *The Psalms: Prayers of Many Moods*. Paulist Press, 1999.

Rogerson, John. *The Psalms in Daily Life*. Paulist Press, 2001.

Stuhlmueller, Carroll, CP. *Psalms* (2 vols.). Liturgical Press, 1983.

14

Prayerful Reading

Many people have found prayerful reading to be a pathway to prayer. This is different from *lectio divina*, discussed elsewhere in this book. That form of prayer is also reading, but it is traditionally limited to the Scriptures, and perhaps the writings of the early Church Fathers.

Whether or not you use the method of *lectio divina* to read the Scriptures slowly and prayerfully, you can do something similar with other spiritual reading. The key is to proceed *slowly*, and to stop whenever you come across a paragraph, a sentence, or even a word that touches your heart. Stay with that thought, that word, as long as the spirit moves you. You might make a note of it in the book, on a separate piece of paper, or in a journal or notebook if you keep one. Roll the thought around in your mind; ask God to help you get the most out of it. And when you are finished (for the moment) with that thought or word, move on.

The key is in the word *slowly*. The idea is not to gain knowledge, nor to get through the book quickly so you can move on to something else. No, the book was written to help you spiritually. It was designed to be read slowly. It was not intended to impart information. It was meant to speak to your heart. Let it.

This can be frustrating to those of us who like to get through lots of books. Many of us do not have that much disposable time; we like to use it efficiently. We would like to be able to read, say, five books instead of only two. We are accustomed to hurrying. But that is what we must not do. And you will surely find that you are rewarded for slowing down the pace.

What books might you read? If you have a spiritual director, you might choose a book which could be discussed with the director. There are literally thousands, and more hit the bookstores every month. Some people find well-written biographies to be excellent fare for reflection. Others are moved by books on prayer, charity, or social justice. You might consider the following:

- *Traditional Classics.* This category includes *The Imitation of Christ,* the writings of St. Teresa of Avila, Cardinal Newman, St. Benedict, St. Thérèse of Lisieux (the Little Flower), and many others.
- *Twentieth-Century Writers.* Americans such as Thomas Merton and Dorothy Day, the Italian-born German priest Romano Guardini, Anglicans C. S. Lewis and Evelyn Underhill, the Dutch priest Henri Nouwen, and Blessed Mother Teresa of Calcutta.
- *Other Current Authors.* Among the many writers who are popular today are Fr. Benedict Groeschel, CFR; Eugene Peterson; Ronald Rolheiser, OMI; Sr. Ruth Burrows, OSB; Richard Rohr, OFM; and the French Canadian Jean Vanier.

The key is to select writers and books that *speak to you.* It does not matter whether they are best-sellers; it does not matter whether the writer is an expert. If you thumb through the pages or read a few of them, you can often tell whether it is "your kind of book." And if you start it and it turns out not to speak to you after all, then close the book and try something else. Your prayer time is too valuable to waste it on finishing a book that is not connecting you to God.

Some Widely Read Books

Ciszek, Walter, SJ. *He Leadeth Me.*
Day, Dorothy. *The Long Loneliness.*
Groeschel, Benedict, CFR. *Listening at Prayer.*
Kempis, Thomas à. *The Imitation of Christ.*
Lewis, C. S. *Mere Christianity.*
Merton, Thomas, OCSO. *The Seven Storey Mountain.*
Newman, John Henry Cardinal. *Parochial and Plain Sermons.*
Nouwen, Henri. *Letters to Marc About Jesus.*
Rolheiser, Ronald, OMI. *The Holy Longing.*
Teresa of Avila, *The Interior Castle.*
Underhill, Evelyn. *The Spiritual Life.*
Vanier, Jean. *Be Not Afraid.*

The books suggested above are all nonfiction, but even novels and poetry can be a source for prayerful reading. You may also wish to consider:

Greene, Graham. *The Heart of the Matter.*
Lewis, C. S. *The Screwtape Letters.*
Robinson, Marilynne. *Gilead.*
Waugh, Evelyn. *Brideshead Revisited.*
West, Morris. *The Shoes of the Fisherman.*

Consider also the series produced by Pauline Books & Media, Poetry as Prayer, which looks at such poets as Jessica Powers, Denise Levertov, and Gerard Manley Hopkins.

For one writer's personal view of the subject, see Nancy M. Malone, *Walking a Literary Labyrinth: A Spirituality of Reading* (Riverhead Trade, 2004).

15

Lectio Divina *as* Daily Prayer

What Is *Lectio Divina?*

This ancient form of prayer, proposed by St. Benedict in the Rule for his monasteries, has been rediscovered only in the last few decades by ordinary Catholics who are not monks or sisters. It is centered on the power of the Word of God to speak to us in our innermost being and call forth a response to Him. This inner conversation of reflection and response leads us to know God's will for us and helps us make the decisions to change and act and grow in our spiritual life.

We need to avoid thinking of reading the Scripture passage as a rational investigation of its meaning for biblical scholarship, and see instead that a slow and attentive reading is the context in which the Holy Spirit speaks to us and moves us to understand God's action in us more deeply. The process of moving from reading to either contemplation or insight into what God calls us to become and do fulfills the spiritual hunger of the modern person who wants to grow in his or her relationship with Jesus and to follow as His disciple more closely in all we do.

Thelma Hall in her wonderful introduction to *lectio divina*, called *Too Deep for Words*, says, "There is no contradiction between contemplation and action. It is like the spring as source and the stream that flows from the spring. We recognize and are in awe at this abundant source of fresh life-giving water, but we also see it flowing out to fertilize the fields and give life to those who drink" (p. 11). She also quotes the words of Jesus in John 7:37–39, "Let anyone who is thirsty come to me...for as Scripture says, 'From his heart will flow streams of living water.' He was speaking of the Spirit which those who believed in him were to receive." Thus both contemplation and action are the work of the Spirit in us as we pray.

The Four Steps of the Prayer

The four steps of *lectio divina* can be called by different names, but are relatively simple as a process:

1. READING THE SCRIPTURES (*LECTIO*)

This is not ordinary reading, but the process of taking a scriptural passage, usually a short one, reading it slowly, and listening to the text and to God's powerful action in it. It speaks to me as the voice of the Holy Spirit at work, and I am reading so as to hear that voice in the text. But it is also intelligent reading, in which we ask: What is the text really about?

2. REFLECTING ON THE TEXT (*MEDITATIO*)

I notice that the words of the text are addressed *to me*. I stop and reflect on one or more aspects of the words that apply to me, in which I see what they describe reflected in my own life and my relationship to God. I enter the text by imagining that I am the subject of these words, or by identifying with the people in the passage, so it moves me to reflect on God's ways in my life.

3. PRAYING WITH THE TEXT (*ORATIO*)

Our meditation on the text is an exercise of our understanding and intellect, and needs to lead to the involvement of our will saying yes to God's word in our lives. That is, it must lead to prayer and to the active commitment in love to God. We take what we have found in this text, open our hearts to accept God's action in our lives, and give ourselves to God, willing to be changed and to give our "yes" in response to His call.

4. CONTEMPLATING (*CONTEMPLATIO*) OR COMMITTING TO ACTION

Two possible outcomes make up our final step of *lectio divina*. One is the passive contemplation of God—becoming absorbed in God's goodness, mercy, and loving presence that He has revealed to us in the steps we have completed. The second is a commitment to a deeper response to God in our lives by actually changing, converting, ourselves to put into action what we have been moved to realize in our reflection and following prayer.

Some Points to Be Noted

READING AS DISCIPLES

It is important to realize that we are reading Scripture as the disciples and siblings of Jesus. His first words of mission announced that the Kingdom of God had come and that all should convert from their sins. Moreover, He taught them that the disciple who would be first must be the servant of all. He showed them that, to follow the Son of Man, they must take up his cross as well. He instructed them in self-surrender—only those who lose their life will find it. He promised them that He would be with them all days, that they would be one with Him, and that the Holy Spirit would instruct them in all that they should do. Finally, He sent them forth to make this Good News known to all peoples. We cannot read any passage of Scripture, Old or New Testament, without having all of these elements of our hope in Christ before our eyes.

CREATING AN ATMOSPHERE OF LISTENING

One must realize from the start that this is a time of prayer, not of book learning—even if the book is the Bible! So we must create quiet time and become silent, so as to "hear" the text, and be aware that God is present and speaking to us. It is not helpful to read slouched in an easy chair with the radio in the background. One should sit upright and lay the Bible before us, so as to read it actively, alert to what will stand out in it for us. An opening prayer acknowledging God's presence would be a good way to start.

LETTING THE SPIRIT SPEAK

It has often been pointed out by psychologists and others that people hear what they want to hear. We can be preoccupied with events that have troubled our day or with issues or ideas that have been bothering us, and bring them into our reading to find the answers we seek. But this is backward. We must try to put aside what has been on our minds, so as to concentrate on letting the text have power and reveal its word to us. What we suddenly start seeing and meditating on may have nothing to do with what has been uppermost in our minds all day, but it will begin the process of changing us from within in new ways we did not expect. On the other hand, we do not want to indulge fanciful dreams that have nothing to do with the real me or my real life and way of thinking. What does this passage say to me about me? How is God speaking to the real me in this?

Lectio Deepens My Relationship with God

We may not believe it, but all of us are at least partially mystics. We can fall in love with God through knowing Him more deeply. All love presupposes knowledge of the beloved; we need to understand that, if we move from reading into prayer and stop to just think about God and how good or great He is, and simply enjoy the moment, that is contemplation. If we come to the conviction that we should make a resolution to act on what we found in the reading, and suddenly find a confident quiet certainty about it that gives us peace, then that too is a form of contemplation. In *lectio divina*, we always come to the realization that we need God to act in us and to strengthen and sustain us. In our final step, then, prayer leads always to accepting God's love for us as the most important value we seek, both in contemplation and in action. The great mystics have much more to say about being drawn into divine love through contemplation, but for daily practice of *lectio divina* we should be content to end always with a short act of love of God that comes from what we have just read, reflected upon, prayed over, and committed to.

As Dietrich Bonhoeffer wrote:

> We ponder the chosen text on the strength of the promise that it has something utterly personal to say to us for this day....Here we are not expounding [the text] or preparing a sermon or conducting Bible study of any kind; we are rather waiting for God's Word to us....Often we are so burdened and overwhelmed with other thoughts, images, and concerns that it may take a long time before God's Word has swept all else aside and come through. But it will surely come. (*Life Together*, Harper [1982], 82)

Further Reading

Casey, Michael, OCSO. *Sacred Reading*. Liguori/Triumph, 1995.

The Catholic Prayer Bible: Lectio Divina Edition (Paulist Press, 2010). This is an excellent Bible created specifically for the prayerful and reflective reading of Scripture.

Hall, Thelma, RC. *Too Deep for Words*. Paulist Press, 1988.

Hough, Stephen. *The Bible as Prayer: A Handbook for Lectio Divina*. Paulist Press, 2007.

See also the comprehensive bibliography and bookstore on the Contemplative Outreach, Ltd. website at www.centeringprayer.com.

16
___

Ignatian Contemplation

Embedded in the *Spiritual Exercises of St. Ignatius of Loyola* (*"SE"*) is a prayer practice widely known as "Ignatian Contemplation." This prayer form has been called an "act of presence": presence to the life of Christ, most often as recounted in Scripture. It aims to help the person at prayer come to a deeply felt response to Christ by being present with Him in the circumstances of His life and by the recognition of Christ's presence in the life of the person at prayer.

It is a relaxed form of prayer since the goal is to be *in* the mystery of Christ's life—to place oneself in the scene and then let the Holy Spirit take over. Fr. John J. English, SJ, describes this form of prayer in his book *Spiritual Freedom*:

> It is also simple.…This approach to prayer requires less mental effort and sets [the person] free, like a bird gliding in the wind. In such an atmosphere the Spirit can move in and out of the person's mind and heart more easily. (p. 132)

This method of prayer makes the events in Scripture present to us and thus engages the heart, exposing us to the love that springs from our encounter with Jesus.

So exactly what does one do to engage in this form of prayer? St. Ignatius gives concrete directions as we are asked to engage our imaginations in the events of Christ's life on earth as depicted in the Scriptures. Conflating the express directions given for the various prayer exercises that make up the course of a full-fledged retreat, the process for this prayer practice generally includes the following points (taken in major part from David L. Fleming, SJ, *Draw Me Into Your Friendship: The Spiritual Exercises: A Literal Translation and A Contemporary Reading*):

Preparation Prayer: Place oneself in God's presence in reverence; beg that everything in one's day be more directed to God's service and praise.

Grace We Ask For: Ask for the grace to know Jesus more intimately, love Him more intensely, and follow Him more closely. We ask for the grace to open our hearts to God's tutelage. We ask for the ability to notice the feelings and desires inspired by our encounter with Jesus.

Scripture Passage: The Scripture passage to be the subject of contemplative prayer is selected; often it is the Gospel for the day. In the Spiritual Exercises, particular passages covering the life of Christ are suggested. One reads the Scripture passage slowly, calling to mind the salient events.

Setting: St. Ignatius calls visualizing the setting of the passage a "composition." We are asked to enter into the whole scene and to be with the persons involved. For example, in the case of the Nativity, St. Ignatius suggests that we enter along the road from Nazareth to Bethlehem, "considering the length and the breath, whether the road is level or through valleys and over hills; likewise looking at the place or cave of the Nativity, how large, how small, how low, how high and how it was prepared" (*SE* 112). We are told to observe carefully each of the people in the scene. Watch how Mary and Joseph handle themselves, their own responses to the labor pains and the miracle of birth. Look on the newborn baby. We are urged to put ourselves into the scene, perhaps as one who is there to help and to serve, an observer, or another participant. Listen to what Mary and Joseph are saying. Take note of the hardships that have already taken place as Jesus' parents struggled to find shelter: their poverty, hunger, thirst, the rejections and insults they have endured, the cold. See their joy and worry. (This same process of "composition" can be used for any Scripture passage.)

Application of the Five Senses: We are specifically directed to see the persons in the scene with "the sight of imagination," to hear what they are or might be saying, as well as all other sounds associated with the event; to smell odors permeating the scene; to taste what, in our imagination, enters our mouths; and to touch and feel the physical aspects of the scene. For example, in the case of the Nativity, we are welcomed to imaginatively pick up and hold the baby Jesus in our arms.

Quiet and the Work of the Spirit: As we enter into the scene fully, we become quiet and open to what strikes us as the scene plays out. We become aware of our feelings and open to lessons that come to us. St. Ignatius taught that we would draw spiritual profit from our reflection on the experience. We prayerfully and reverently relish God's presence with us. The result might be challenging and disturbing, or elevating and exciting. The Holy Spirit is at work with us.

Colloquy: We are invited to respond in prayerful conversation with Jesus, God the Father, the Holy Spirit, Mary, or others in a particular scene, as however we are moved. This is the time to discuss in conversation what happened during the prayer period. Bring the period of prayerful conversation to a close with an Our Father.

Review of Prayer: After the exercise or time of prayer is over, Ignatius suggests a short reflection on the prayer experience itself. Look back and think about it. What happened in the time of prayer? What were the good things or the disturbing things in the prayer? Keep notes for yourself in a journal.

The same imaginative faculty that enables us to enter personally into the world of a stunning work of art, moving piece of music or poem, good novel, movie, or stage play here helps us to contemplate Christ's life in a vivid and compelling way. We listen and discover what God is saying to us. Inspired by the Holy Gospel in this unique way, we meet God in these events and are moved to return to daily life with enthusiasm and charity. The encounter of God through the imagination provokes feelings of gratitude, which in turn prompt one's desires to follow Jesus, and to proclaim, and further live for, God's intention for love and beauty to flourish in the world.

Further Reading

English, John J., SJ. *Spiritual Freedom*, 2nd ed. Loyola Press, 1995.

Fleming, David L., SJ. *Draw Me into Your Friendship: The Spiritual Exercises: A Literal Translation and Contemporary Reading*. Institute of Jesuit Sources, 1996.

Introduction to Ignatian Prayer at www.prayerwindows.com/Ignatian.html.

Martin, James, SJ. *The Jesuit Guide to (Almost) Everything*. HarperCollins, 2010.

17

The Daily Examen

How do things stand between God and me? Where am I coming from, and where is my life in Christ growing? We can answer these questions satisfactorily only if we take time to reflect.

Ignatian Tradition

St. Ignatius of Loyola believed that we can find God in all things and at every moment, even in the most ordinary. The Daily Examen of St. Ignatius is a time of restful prayer when we review and evaluate the hours of our day in the light of faith. We prayerfully reflect on our experience since the last Examen. St. Ignatius considered this prayer the most important spiritual exercise for his men, his fellow Jesuits, and encouraged them to pray the Examen each day if nothing else. For his men, it has made a singular difference.

Chris Lowney explores the keys to successful leadership in his book about the Jesuits, *Heroic Leadership: Best Practices from a 450-year-old Company That Changed the World*. What he says about leaders really applies to everyone: "Leaders thrive by understanding who they are and what they value, by becoming aware of unhealthy blind spots or weaknesses that can derail them, and by cultivating the habit of continuous self-reflection and learning" (p. 27). He marvels at the array of tools and practices the Jesuits invented, adopted, and employed to mold that self-awareness and secure in their members the habit of continuous self-reflection. A key practice, perhaps the most important, was and is the Daily Examen.

A Regular Practice

Jesuits, and now others, both lay and religious, affirm that the Examen is an essential part of the spiritual and apostolic inheritance from St. Ignatius. He directed his men to pause each day in a contemplative way, to give thanks to God, and then to ask for God's light. This regular prayer exercise surfaces significant, affirming, or disturbing events that marked the day. It makes us more aware of how much God's grace has touched us. It also calls us to account by posing the threefold question: "What have I done for Christ? What am I doing for Christ? What ought I do for Christ?"

The Daily Examen traditionally takes about ten to twenty minutes (although if time is lacking, this may be shortened) and is done daily at a convenient time toward the end of the day. It is helpful to plan a definite time for this prayer and to keep a journal of the fruits of prayer and the insights gained.

Traditionally the Daily Examen involves five steps. What follows is adapted from the description of the Daily Examen found in *Hearts on Fire: Praying with the Jesuits*, edited by Michael Harter, SJ, and in *St. Ignatius' Prayer of Awareness: The Examen: The Five Steps of the Daily Examen* by Kevin J. O'Brien, SJ.

1. Thanksgiving

Take time to thank God for the good things that came into the day. Review the many details of the day. Find one thing to be thankful for—even if you are having a tough time. Allow gratitude to take hold of you.

2. Pray for Insight

Pray to the Holy Spirit to reveal to you what you need at this time. In conversation, ask God to help you be grateful and honest as you look at the day. With God's help, be attentive to how the Spirit was working in and through you and within creation. Consciously open yourself to God's light.

3. Finding God in All Things

This is the heart of the prayer, where you examine very concretely the events of the day. It is like playing a DVD or videocassette of the day. Review the day and then name the blessings, from the significant to the most ordinary. Hit the pause button when something stands out. Recall the details. Be specific. Savor the gifts that God shows you and note feelings of discomfort when they arise.

St. Ignatius taught that God communicates with us not only through mental insight, but also through what he called "our interior movements": our feelings, emotions, desires, attractions, repulsions, and moods. As you play back the day, you may notice some strong feelings arising. They may be painful or pleasing: for example, joy, peace, sadness, anxiety, confusion, hope, compassion, regret, anger, confidence, jealousy, self-doubt, boredom, or excitement. Feelings themselves are neither positive nor negative. It is what we do with them that raises moral questions. These "movements" can tell us a lot about the direction of our lives.

Pick one or two strong feelings or "movements" and pray from them. Ask God to help you to understand what aroused those feelings and where they led you:

- Did they draw you to God?
- Did they help you grow in faith, hope, and love?
- Did they make you more generous with your time and talent?
- Did they make you feel more alive, whole, and human?
- Did they lead you to feel more connected to others or challenge you to life-giving growth?

Or—

- Did they lead you away from God; make you less faithful, hopeful, or loving?
- Did they cause you to become more self-centered or anxious?
- Did they lure you into doubt and confusion?
- Did they lead to breakdown in relationships?

Sometimes no particular action or event will stand out, but you might find a pattern emerging in the day. Patiently, ask yourself what a pattern might mean about your trust in or love for God.

This review is a chance to take a step back and recognize that God is active in the entirety of the day.

4. Prayerful Conversation with God

Take what you learned to prayer, speak to God, and tell God whatever you need to say. Rejoice in the times you were brought closer to God, and ask for forgiveness for the times you resisted God's power in your life today. Let God surprise you with insight and console you with faith and hope.

5. Look to Tomorrow

Finally, look ahead. Invite God to be a part of your future. Express to God your desires. Again, be specific and frame your prayer in a petition, as here:

> Dear Lord, at this time I ask for the grace of [...], for the strength to [...], for courage to [...], for the resolve to [...], to be thankful for [...], and so on.

Determine to keep your spirit filled with gratitude, and take steps to get rid of mindsets that stand between you and your Creator. Close with a prayer speaking to God from the heart or with a familiar prayer like the Our Father, the Prayer of St. Ignatius ("Take, Lord, and Receive"), or the Prayer of St. Francis of Assisi.

Dennis Hamm, SJ, gave an outstanding, concise explanation of the Examen in his article "Rummaging for God: Praying Backward Through the Day," originally published in *America* magazine, May 1994.

The Examen is a wonderfully simple and effective prayer practice of reviewing the day to see and relive the occasions of grace and to note those areas where improvement is called for. This daily review, beginning as it does in gratitude for the benefits and graces received, opens our eyes so we can live and act in the present, where God wants us to work with Him for the good of all His creation, so that His Kingdom of love, peace, and justice will come.

Further Reading

Aschenbrenner, George, SJ. *Consciousness Examen.* Loyola Press, 2007.

Hamm, Dennis, SJ. "Rummaging for God: Praying Backward Through the Day, from *America Magazine,* May 1994, found at http://onlineministries.creighton.edu/colla borativeministry/audioretreat/hamm-2009/. At the bottom of the web page, click on the link to the article.

Harter, Michael, SJ, ed. *Hearts on Fire: Praying with Jesuits.* The Institute of Jesuit Sources, 1993.

Lowney, Chris. *Heroic Leadership: Best Practices from a 450-Year-Old Company That Changed the World.* Loyola, 1995.

Roccosalvo, Joan L., CSJ. *Prayer for Finding God in All Things: The Daily Examen of St. Ignatius of Loyola.* The Institute of Jesuit Sources, 2005.

18
___

Centering Prayer
The Prayer of Quiet

Note to the reader and "pray-er"

The two descriptions of CENTERING PRAYER and CONTEM-
PLATIVE PRAYER that follow should be read and considered together because they address our part in prayer
disposing us to God's part, His gift in our prayer time and
at other times throughout the day. However, Teresa of
Avila and John of the Cross caution us that these steps
are not to be understood as occurring in a strictly linear
fashion but rather as continually overlapping and recurring in cycles. These two sections define and describe
Centering Prayer and contemplative prayer, and attempt
to show how they relate to one another.

Centering Prayer is a quiet time with God, which can sometimes—with God's grace—lead to what is called contemplative prayer. Other approaches to God, such as those in this
book, can also end up as contemplative prayer. But unlike
these other approaches, Centering Prayer is a grace—a gift
from God—and is not accomplished solely by an act of the
will. It defies formula. But the following is an attempt to
convey some aspects of this gift from God.

We begin by acknowledging that prayer is principally
God's work and God's gift. What has been our part in prayer

throughout the ages? In *Open Mind, Open Heart,* Father Thomas Keating answers by characterizing Centering Prayer as:

> an effort to renew the teaching of the Christian tradition on contemplative prayer that characterized the first fifteen centuries of the Christian era but had become marginalized over the next centuries. It is an attempt to present that tradition in an up-to-date form and to put a certain order and method into it. Like the word *contemplation,* the term *Centering Prayer* has come to have a variety of meanings. For the sake of clarity it seems best to reserve the term *Centering Prayer* for the specific method of preparing for the gift of contemplation.

In Centering Prayer, we become "quiet." This prepares us to enter into contemplative prayer, which is a prayer of "union" with God. Some call Centering Prayer a "level" of contemplative prayer. Others refer to it as a discipline designed to withdraw our attention from the ordinary flow of our thoughts. It opens our awareness to the spiritual level of our being. It is a method designed to facilitate the development of contemplative prayer by preparing our faculties to cooperate with this gift of infused contemplation. Perhaps it can be viewed as "setting the stage" for entering into contemplative prayer. The principal effects of Centering Prayer are experienced in daily life, not in the period of Centering Prayer itself. Centering Prayer, or the Prayer of Quiet, may go on for years. It is an effort to renew the teaching of the Christian tradition on contemplative prayer. It is not contemplative prayer; it is distinct from *lectio divina,* which is a method for communing with God that begins with the reading of a passage from Scripture. The heart and soul of Centering Prayer is consent to the presence and action of God in our lives.

During the time of prayer, it centers one's attention on God's presence and action within. At other times, one's attention moves outward to discover His presence everywhere else. Centering Prayer is not an end in itself, but a beginning. It is not done for the sake of having an experience, but for the sake of its positive fruits in one's life.

Thomas Keating describes the role of Centering Prayer as a method designed to facilitate the development of contemplative prayer by preparing our faculties to cooperate with this gift. He stresses that rather than replacing other kinds of prayer, Centering Prayer puts them into a new and fuller perspective.

The following composite of summaries by Keating and Carl Arico clarifies what Centering Prayer *is* and *is not*:

CENTERING PRAYER IS *not*

- a technique
- a relaxation exercise
- a form of self-hypnosis
- a charismatic gift
- a para-psychological experience
- something limited to the "felt" presence of God
- discursive meditation or affective prayer
- something we accomplish on our own

CENTERING PRAYER *is*

- a relationship with God and, at the same time, a discipline to foster that relationship
- an exercise of faith, hope, and love
- a movement beyond conversation to communion with Christ
- a cultivation of language of God, which is silence
- simple attentiveness to the divine presence

The following is a summary of the guidelines for the Centering Prayer method. Full explanations and many practical points can be found in books by Keating and Arico listed at the end of this chapter.

1. Choose a sacred word as the symbol of your intention to consent to God's presence and action within (e.g., *Kyrie*, Abba, Jesus, Silence, Amen).
2. Sitting comfortably and with eyes closed, settle briefly, and silently introduce the sacred word as the symbol of your consent to God's presence and action within.
3. When you become aware of thoughts, return ever so gently to the sacred word.
4. At the end of the prayer period, remain in silence with eyes closed for a couple of minutes.

Among the practical points Keating and Arico suggest include a recommendation that the minimum time for this prayer is twenty minutes and a recommendation of two periods each day, one at the beginning and one at the end of the day.

There are also some practices that can help maintain the interior silence throughout the day and extend its effects in our ordinary activities. The following checklist is taken from Fr. Keating's *Open Mind, Open Heart*:

1. *Cultivate a basic acceptance of yourself.* You need to have compassion for yourself and your failings and limitations. You will make many mistakes, but you can learn from them.
2. *Pick a prayer for action.* Choose a short sentence from scripture—five to nine syllables works best—and repeat it to yourself throughout the

day, even during menial tasks. Eventually the prayer will work itself into your subconscious and will "say itself."

3. *Spend time daily listening to the Word of God in lectio divina.* At least fifteen minutes a day with the New Testament or another book that speaks to your heart is recommended. This practice ties into other chapters of this book.

4. *Carry a "minute book."* One of Keating's most interesting recommendations is to jot down in a small notebook a sentence or two—at most, a paragraph—from your favorite spiritual writers or from your own journal. Carry it with you and read a few lines when you have the chance.

5. *Deliberately dismantle the emotional programming of the false self.* Determine the emotions that most upset you—and that thereby disturb your interior silence. What are their triggers? By a strong act of the will, release the desires that underlie these emotions, such as, "I give up my desire for (security, esteem, control)!" If you can prevent these emotional "programs" from going off, your Centering Prayer will be far more effective.

6. *Practice "guard of the heart."* Keating says to release upsetting emotions into the present moment. This can be done by focusing on what you are currently doing, turning your attention to another activity, or giving the feeling to Christ. Whichever you do, you will need to let go of your personal likes or dislikes. The fruit of this practice will be a willingness to change your plans at a moment's notice.

7. *Practice unconditional acceptance of others.* If other people's actions and idiosyncrasies disturb you, try to let go and accept others as they are. If you feel the need to correct them (which usually gets you nowhere when you are upset and they are defensive), it is better to wait until you are calm, and then offer correction out of genuine concern for them.

8. *Deliberately dismantle excessive group identification.* Like many of us, you may be tied too tightly to your groups. This prevents you from being open to change, including spiritual change. This means letting go of the preconceptions that keep us too closely bound to our groups.

9. *Celebrate the Eucharist regularly.* Stay close to this mystery, the source of all Christian transformation.

10. *Join a contemplative prayer group.* Few can make these transformative changes without the support of others who are struggling along the same path. Set up a group, or join one that already meets weekly. There is much more on this topic in the chapter of this book on faith-sharing groups.

The Value of a Support Group

Small prayer groups are discussed elsewhere in this book. The spontaneity of the early Christian communities described by Paul and in the Acts of the Apostles is being rediscovered in our time. While Centering Prayer is done privately most of the time, a weekly sharing of the experience in a small group (up to fifteen) has proven to be very supportive, as well as a means of continuing education. By sharing the experience of Centering Prayer with others, one's own discernment of the ups and downs of the practice is sharpened. The group serves as a source of encouragement and can normally solve problems that might arise regarding the method.

Further Reading

PRAYER

Arico, C. *A Taste of Silence: A Guide to the Fundamentals of Centering Prayer.* Continuum, 1999.
Keating, Thomas A., OCSO. *Open Mind, Open Heart: The Contemplative Dimension of the Gospel,* pp. 168–71. Continuum, 1986, 1992, 2002.

PRAYER GROUP

Underhill, E. *The Fruits of the Spirit,* Part II, pp. 43–72. Longmans, Green and Co., 1942.

INFORMATION/PAMPHLETS/RETREATS

Contemplative Outreach Ltd. International Office
10 Park Place Suite 2-B
P.O. Box 737
Butler, NJ 07405
Phone: (973) 838-3384
Fax: (973) 492-5795
www.centeringprayer.com

19

Contemplative Prayer
The Prayer of Union

Contemplative prayer is a resting in God's presence. It is the opening of the mind and heart—the whole being—to God, the Ultimate Mystery, beyond thoughts, words, and emotions. In the end, all words are inadequate as we enter into the mystery of God, whose first language is silence. As Thomas Merton says, "My prayer, then, is a kind of praise, rising up out of the center of nothingness and silence." The contemplative journey is essentially one of surrender. St. John of the Cross says that our personal death is the ultimate moment of contemplation because we finally surrender everything to be present to God. Thomas Keating says that contemplative prayer is a process of interior transformation, a conversation initiated by God and leading, if we consent, to divine union. In the contemplative world, God is loved above every creature, purely and simply for Himself. For the contemplative, the work of love by itself will eventually heal. Contemplative prayer removes the roots of sin and begins a deeper healing process.

Contemplative prayer is bestowed in God's own way and in God's own time; it has no roots in human intent or effort except for the deep and secret welcoming, the "yes" that we say, sometimes unaware. It is a gift that can come to anyone.

Passive purification is one of the fruits of the gift of contemplation. God is the active agent. The creature needs to be receptive—what God the Creator does is more important. The gift of contemplation brings us into God's territory, so to speak, on God's terms, beyond our ordinary way of seeing and hearing what is involved. Merton notes that it is not an escape from conflict, anguish, or doubt. Another gift or fruit of contemplation is an ability to let go of control, esteem, and security.

Contemplative prayer is a preparation for action that emerges from the inspiration of the Spirit in the silencing of our own agitation, desires, and hang-ups. Such silence gives God the maximum opportunity to speak.

Contemplative prayer fosters an entirely different attitude toward one's feelings; it puts them in a different frame of reference. Most extreme feelings come from a sense of insecurity, especially when we feel threatened. But when you are being constantly reaffirmed by the presence of God in deep silence, you are not afraid of being contradicted or imposed upon. You might be humble enough to learn something from insults and humiliations without being overwhelmed by feelings of self-deprecation or revenge. Negative feelings toward oneself tend to be prevalent in our culture due to the low self-image people develop in early childhood, possibly because of our highly competitive society. Anyone who does not win feels that he or she is no good in this culture, whereas in the quiet of deep prayer, you are a new person, or rather, you are you.

Contemplative prayer changes the way one sees reality. Centering Prayer is a rung on the ladder to contemplative prayer. It is a method of moving our developing relationship with God to the level of pure faith. Pure faith moves beyond our active efforts at meditation and other prayers to the intuitive level of contemplation. Contemplative prayer is the way of pure faith. Nothing else. You do not have to feel it but you do have to practice it. It is the world in which God can do anything. To move into that realm is the greatest adventure. It is to be open to the Infinite and hence to infinite possibilities. A new world appears within and around us and the impossible becomes an everyday experience. It is an experience or series of experiences leading to the abiding state of union with God.

One of the first effects of contemplative prayer is the release of the energies of the unconscious. There are two psychological states: (1) spiritual consolation, charismatic gifts, or psychic powers (which can give rise to pride); and (2) the experience of human weakness through humiliating self-knowledge, the consciousness of one's dark side (which can give rise to discouragement or despair). We need to cultivate habits of dedication to God and service to others to stabilize the mind in the face of emotionally charged thoughts, whether self-exaltation or self-deprecation.

Contemplation is a gift of God, the knowledge of God that is impregnated with love. It is a resting in God.

The value of contemplative prayer is that it is a total immersion in that aspect of our relationship to God that happens to be the most important—the cultivation of interior silence. The chief work in contemplative prayer is to receive God; it is an act of the will that is not effort but surrender.

Contemplative prayer opens you to the power of the Spirit. Your capacity to keep giving all day long will increase. You will be able to adjust to difficult circumstances and even to live with impossible situations.

Contemporary Western minds are so active that, in practicing contemplative prayer, many people need to repeat a Christian mantra over and over, at least in the beginning.

People leading very active lives can certainly benefit from that sort of concentration to hold their attention. This is the great battle in the early stages of Centering Prayer—the battle with thoughts.

If you habitually practice Centering Prayer, you will find that the amount of interior noise is gradually reduced. Try to ignore the ordinary wanderings of the imagination. Bear in mind that God's first language is silence. The time devoted to interior silence is not meant to be in conflict with other forms of prayer. There is a reciprocal interaction between your activity during the day and your prayer, and vice versa. They mutually support one another.

In summary, the following lists include the essential components or characteristics of the Prayer of Quiet (Centering Prayer) and the Prayer of Union (contemplation):

CENTERING PRAYER is

- what seems to be our own doing
- what we do intentionally using the faculties of intellect, memory, and will
- a focused practice
- something we choose

CONTEMPLATION is

- what seems to come as a sheer gift
- what cannot be practiced
- something that is entirely God's gift of grace
- an experience that is open and unfocused "in the now"

These two types of prayer have been discussed sequentially and could be mistakenly perceived as a progression. It is important to reemphasize that they do not necessarily occur that way.

Further Reading

BOOKS

Keating, Thomas. A., OCSO. *Open Mind, Open Heart: The Contemplative Dimension of the Gospel.* Continuum, 1986, 1992, 2002.

Merton, Thomas, OCSO. *Contemplative Prayer.* Image Books, Doubleday, 1971.

Spoto, Donald. *In Silence: Why We Pray.* Penguin, 2004.

INFORMATION/PAMPHLETS/RETREATS

Contemplative Outreach Ltd. International Office
10 Park Place Suite 2-B
P.O. Box 737
Butler, NJ 07405
Phone: (973) 838-3384
Fax: (973) 492-5795
www.centeringprayer.com

20

Spiritual Direction

Spiritual direction is among the many traditional practices in the Church that encourage prayer and help develop the soul of the individual in his or her pilgrimage toward Christ. Spiritual direction focuses on helping the person deepen their relationship with God—not so much to understand the relationship as to enter into it, to engage in it, to enter into conversation with God about daily life. Spiritual direction is concerned with what happens when a person listens to and responds to God.

The spiritual director is an individual trained to walk with the person, to accompany the person on his or her faith journey. The well-trained and experienced director will listen to the person's prayer experiences and help clarify what God is saying and doing in the relationship. The primary relationship is always between God and the person; the director is a privileged companion. Spiritual direction is not psychological counseling, pastoral counseling, or the sacrament of Reconciliation. It is about one's relationship with God and how that relationship is exercised in prayer.

Spiritual direction has increased tremendously in popularity worldwide since the 1970s; it is no longer reserved for the ordained but is enjoying widespread appeal among the laity. Similarly, more clergy, more women and men religious, and more laypersons have been trained in the practice and art of spiritual direction. Today, because there are so many spiritual directors, it is important to insure that the spiritual director you might ask to be a companion on the journey be trained and compatible with you as a person.

As one tries to turn serious attention to prayer, the individual will invariably encounter significant obstacles. As just one example, spiritual direction has historically suffered from the mistaken conception that directees should unreservedly follow the advice of a director. Perhaps there is a basic misunderstanding about the whole Christian mystery, or a resistance to change, or a fear of some kind, or other forms of subconscious self-protection. These obstacles are part of our humanity.

Thomas Merton's Approach

Thomas Merton offers some practical advice. He does not assume that everyone needs direction; he states that the young need it more than the old, but that each case is different. For anyone who does need it, direction can assist his or her soul in the life in Christ. Merton's 1959 book *Spiritual Direction and Meditation* offers an accessible guide to this topic. In this work he addresses the meaning and purpose of direction, its necessity, how one should best profit by it, and the centrality of the manifestation of one's conscience during direction.

Merton describes spiritual direction as "a continuous process of formation and guidance, in which the Christian is led and encouraged in his special vocation so that by faithful correspondence with the graces of the Holy Spirit he may attain to the particular end of his vocation and to union with God." He notes that the purpose of spiritual direction is "to penetrate beneath the surface of a man's life...and to bring out his inner spiritual freedom, his inmost truth, which is what we call the likeness of Christ in his soul." In their 1982 book, *The Practice of Spiritual Direction*, William A. Barry, SJ, and William J. Connolly, SJ, define *spiritual direction* as "help given by one Christian to another which enables that person to pay attention to God's personal communication to him or her, to respond to this personally communicating with God, to grow in intimacy with God, and to live out the consequences of the relationship."

Spiritual direction presupposes an active faith, a deep spiritual hunger, and a capacity for serious reflection. As one's response to a spiritual appetite is taking shape, spiritual direction can serve as a "safeguard against deformation." Spiritual direction, Merton writes, is "concerned with the whole person not simply as an individual, but as a son of God, seeking to recover the perfect likeness to God in Christ." The director helps to recognize and to follow the inspirations of grace in his or her life. Flannery O'Connor recognized the difficulty of responding to grace when she wrote, "Human nature vigorously resists grace because grace changes us and the change is painful."

Merton portrays our contemporary situation quite well, but may be unrealistic in some places. For example, he states that ordinary Christian laypeople may not find direction necessary because their needs would usually be met by the pastor or regular parish confessor. The kind of direction ordinarily available would be inseparable from the sacrament of Confession and would be quite adequate for most individuals, says Merton. But many laypeople have profited from spiritual direction outside of Confession.

Merton describes dedicated spiritual direction, which is his essay's concern, as going much deeper and aiming at the orientation of one's life for those with a special vocation or apostolic mission in view. Certainly he regards it as obligatory for vowed religious and recommended for those lay individuals with a special work for the Church. He writes, "Even though it may not be strictly necessary, it is always useful." He also notes that some "pious souls" take their "spiritual lives" too seriously and pay exaggerated attention to their "progress." The wise director will help these individuals with their self-preoccupation and focus them on God and on others. He notes that essential to the process of spiritual direction is a normal, spontaneous human relationship.

Merton's comments on the necessity of the manifestation of conscience are perhaps his most insightful. The manifestation of conscience may be more difficult than the confession of sins with the opening up of the basic attitudes of the soul to another. He advises those undergoing spiritual direction to bring the director into contact with one's real self, letting go of unconscious efforts to maintain a façade. He mentions the temptation to embellish one's material for the director so that one's case or problem is interesting. He describes the tendency for self-defense and self-justification as being the greatest impediment to grace in this setting. In addition, he reviews the common pitfalls of one undergoing direction.

Merton also refers to the wisdom of the spiritual director and recalls the words of St. Teresa of Avila to her community:

> Give great praise to God, Daughters, for this liberty that you have, for, though there are not a great many priests whom you can consult, there are a few, other than your ordinary confessors, who can give you light upon everything. I beg every superior, for the love of the Lord, to allow a holy liberty here: let the Bishop or

Provincial he approached for leave for the sisters to go from time to time beyond their ordinary confessors and talk about their souls with persons of learning, especially if the confessors, though good men, have no learning; for learning is a great help in giving light upon everything. It should be possible to find a number of people who combine both learning and spirituality, and the more favors the Lord grants you in prayer, the more needful is it that your good works and your prayers should have a sure foundation....You might suppose that any confessor would know this, but you would be wrong: it happened that I had to go about matters of conscience to a man who had taken a complete course in theology; and he did me a great deal of mischief by telling me that certain things were of no importance. I know that he had no intention of deceiving me, or any reason for doing so: it was simply that he knew no better. And in addition to this instance I have met with two or three similar ones.

Henri Nouwen and Dorothy Day

Henri Nouwen, in his book *Spiritual Direction*, notes that living a spiritual life takes time and a commitment to create space for God in our lives. He cites the three classic spiritual practices as particularly useful for spiritual direction: interior prayer, *lectio divina* (the sacred reading of the Scriptures and other spiritual writings), and the discipline of the Church (see the other chapters on these topics). Nouwen argues that meeting with a spiritual director allows for focused conversations on how our individual lives are "a part of the great, unfolding story of God's people."

Also should look to the example of Dorothy Day, who wrote:

As a convert I can say these things, knowing how many times I turned away, almost in disgust, from the idea of God and giving myself up to Him. I know the feeling of uneasiness, of weariness, the feeling of strain put upon the soul from driving it, instead of abandoning it to God. And how anyone can persist in the search for God without the assistance of the Church and the advice of hers, with the experience of generations behind them, I do not know.

How Spiritual Direction "Works"

You need to find a director and arrange a regular schedule with him or her; most directors will meet with you monthly or even more frequently. A parish priest could be a possibility, or a priest who is a member of a religious order. While in the past, people often expected a spiritual director to be a priest, this no longer need be the case. Women religious and lay men and women—if they have the gift and the training—can be wonderful guides. Finding the right person is not always easy, but you should not be bashful about asking. And if no person of your acquaintance seems to be appropriate—ask around to find out whom other friends and acquaintances might recommend or suggest.

Depending on your director's availability, you might find yourself meeting monthly (or more or less frequently) for perhaps an hour. You will review your spiritual (and daily) life for the past month, and receive advice, perhaps recommendations for spiritual readings or other practices. If your director is a priest, you might conclude with Confession.

The Church offers us the practice of spiritual direction in order to assist us with our life in Christ. It can be an essential guide and help to prayer.

References

Barry, William A., SJ, and William J. Connolly, SJ. *The Practice of Spiritual Direction*. HarperCollins, 1982.

Day, Dorothy. "Letter to an Agnostic," *The Catholic Worker* 5 (August 4, 1934): 390.

Merton, Thomas, OCSO. *Spiritual Direction and Meditation*. Liturgical Press, 1960.

Nouwen, Henri. *Spiritual Direction*. Harper Collins, 2006.

O'Connor, Flannery. *Spiritual Writings*. Orbis Books, 2003, p. 18.

St. Teresa of Avila. *Way of Perfection*, chapter 5.

Further Reading

Barry, William A., SJ. *Spiritual Direction and the Encounter with God: A Theological Inquiry*. Paulist Press, 2004.

Bloom, Anthony. *Beginning to Pray*. Paulist Press, 1970.

Brother Lawrence. *The Practice of the Presence of God*. Revell, 1885.

Edwards, Tilden. *Spiritual Friend: Reclaiming the Gift of Spiritual Direction*. Paulist Press, 1980.

LaPlace, Jean. *Preparing for Spiritual Direction*. Franciscan Herald Press, 1975.

Leech, Kenneth. *Soul Friend: A Study of Spirituality*. Sheldon Press, 1977.

Merton, Thomas, OCSO. *Contemplative Prayer*. Herder and Herder, 1969.

Steindl-Rast, Brother David, OSB. *Gratefulness, the Heart of Prayer: An Approach to Life in Fullness*. Paulist Press, 1984.

21

Faith-Sharing Groups

Father of light from whom every good gift comes,
send your Spirit into our lives with the power of a
    mighty wind
and by the flame of your wisdom,
open the horizons of our minds.
    (Alternate Opening Prayer, Pentecost Sunday)

Sharing Faith

Common to all of us is the need to reflect—on our faith, our lives, our relationships with God, our relationship with others, our decisions, and our actions. We have lots to do, but we need to reflect on *what* we are doing. We bring a lifetime, *our* lifetime, of rich experiences and spiritual thinking to our reflection. These reflections may be fleeting; they may quietly become the underpinnings of one's private times of silence. And they may be shared with others.

Many find it helpful and rewarding to join with others with similar backgrounds and interest to seek wisdom and understanding. A small-group setting can provide an appealing format in the search for comprehension of the countless parameters of our lives. It gives one a pretext, sometimes needed by busy people, to find, to pause, to reflect, to grow.

The Church's Renew Program

The Church initiated a contemporary interest in small groups decades ago with the Renew program. Many of the participants in those structured groups found them to be a source of enrichment for their prayer and daily lives. Many continued to meet and to discuss spiritual subjects well after the formal end of the program. They had found like-minded "companions on the journey" who helped enhance their lives grounded in faith.

Types of Faith-Sharing Groups

Many different kinds of groups exist. Variations include the number of participants, type of format and discussions, and the length and frequency of meetings. Different groups choose different faith-related books, recordings, and other resources to discuss. Prayer is integral to the process.

In many small groups, members participate in a more informal process. Meeting times, frequency, and location are democratically decided. Different topics characterize different groups. Some base their discussions on the coming week's Sunday Mass readings. Many resources are readily available to aid in the exegesis of Scripture, organized on the liturgical calendar. Such information is frequently provided to lectors by their churches. Other groups center their topics on Scripture, on contemporary writers of spiritual or theological subjects, on Vatican II documents (especially *Lumen Gentium*), or on ecclesial situations of interest to the group. Prayer, reflection, and the sharing of experiences round out the meeting.

Practical Considerations

The practical aspects for a small group are, first of all, finding those who would like and be able to participate in such an endeavor on a regular basis, such as once or twice a month, and those who are actively interested in growing in faith and understanding.

Group membership is usually gained by either of two ways: receiving an invitation to join an existing group, or inviting others to join a group or found a new one. Shared backgrounds—especially of faith, education, and interests—lead to compatibility and longevity of groups. Each person brings individual characteristics but comes from the common bond of a life of faith, and shares a desire to learn, contemplate, react, and relate experiences, with the goal of strengthening their faith life. Respect for the other participants and for the context of discussions is vital and key to growth. The continuity of the group is prized by its fortunate participants but, hopefully, not to the extent of excluding new membership. The group as a whole should decide about new membership, preferably with a welcoming stance; new participants frequently bring new life and interest and are beneficial to any group.

Participating in opening and closing prayer is an important part of the faith grounding. Discussion should be limited in topic and length, such as a short passage of Scripture, a chapter of a book of spirituality being read by all, the examination of issues strengthening or undermining a life of faith, or spirit-based solutions to the knotty problems of life universal to all. Meeting on a regular basis with a small compatible core group can be of great worth in seeking understanding of our life's mission.

Usually, there are certain levels of preparation necessary to enhance any discussion, such as reading the next agreed-upon text selection, locating a scriptural reference, and contemplating an upcoming topic. Often members assume leadership of the group on a rotation basis. The role of the leader is to guide—not to control.

The sharing of one's personal experiences is usually an important part of small-group dynamics (with the caveat that the sharing time is built in and does not take over the meeting). Such sharing testifies that, over time, trust has developed; often opinions are asked and valued. Friendships that last a lifetime can originate in a small faith-sharing group.

How often to meet? This will vary with the group's commitment and availability. Some groups meet weekly, others monthly, some in between. It seems that most groups would not derive comparable benefits from meeting less frequently than once a month.

The Compatibility Factor

The functioning of each group is distinct, with some providing a welcoming atmosphere and others not. Some spark a glint of understanding akin to the New Testament spiritual companionship of Paul and Barnabas. However, as with any group, different personalities may not be at ease with each other, the subject matter may not be of interest, the level of comfort may not lead to spirit-filled, open discussion. Each individual group has its own personality. It is worth exploring several groups, in seeking out the right mixture of compatibility, as well as the appropriate type and level of material covered.

A welcoming atmosphere is conducive to developing respect, trust, and confidence in being able to express ideas, bring up questions, have differing opinions, and discuss sensitive issues. A sense of confidentiality is an important part of sharing and trusting. If one is not at ease and, after deep reflection, sees no chance for change within oneself or the group, it is best to withdraw and continue searching for the right mixture. Groups of many different natures, goals, and levels of spirituality do exist.

Benefits and Blessings

The fostering of an awareness of God's gifts and presence in one's life is part of one's vocation, as is the awareness of returning such gifts to God. To actively participate, to join with others in a private environment, to seek understanding, to reflect on the place of Scripture and Church teachings in our active lives—all of these enhance the understanding of one's own life in God and one's place with others.

"Theological Reflection"—Innovative Approach to Group Sharing

There is major growing interest both in academic circles and in the wider faith community for the dynamic approach to group sharing called theological reflection. Its particular strength is the integration of faith and life. This method is gaining respect for being clearly focused, being resistant to subject drift, and staying on track with the major issues. Theological reflection is being adopted to help "us reflect in ways that allow faith to touch our lives and our lives to touch our faith."[1]

The process, which has a strong intellectual component, sets three key sources into interaction with one another: *experience* (acknowledging the multiplicity of factors that intersect at a particular place in our lives); *authentic tradition* (including Scripture, authoritative documents, and history); and *culture* (our daily lives lived in our current conflicted environments). These provide the base.

The meetings are led by a trained facilitator and begin with prayer. Usually related written materials are made available. The participants explore points of agreement and inconsistencies among the three key sources as relating to issues important in their lives: "How does my experience resonate with Scripture?" "Which is a more powerful influence in my life—faith or secular values?"

The theological-reflection format critiques culture and recognizes ways in which culture could be undermining discipleship. The process examines actual choices that we face in daily life, in our concrete actions, and in events. It identifies points of agreement or conflict between or among the three key resources. It promotes a better understanding of what's right, rather than trying to prove right or wrong. It helps people look at culture from the view of faith and understands how culture sometimes makes actions that are in line with Christ's teaching the more difficult to carry out.

The goal is to explore and understand competing issues rather than debating them. It seeks a greater understanding of the intertwining nature of all parts of our lives. With this setting and process, there is no debate or attempt at persuasion, but there is a gradual, rational accumulation of factors from the relevant key sources. The participants reach a broader understanding of aspects of their lives relating to such issues as "How is God calling me to be faithful?" and "How can I connect my faith and my daily life?"

When this process is carefully carried out, reasonable dialogue prevails over negative reaction or embittered debate. The dynamics of the method are well-shepherded by the trained facilitator. Such training in the theological reflection process is available at lay educational institutions (such as, in Washington and Virginia, the EPS program at Trinity University in Washington, DC). [2]

Notes

1. Joye Gros, *Theological Reflection Connecting Faith and Life,* Loyola Press, 2001.

2. The EPS main office is located at Trinity University, Michigan Ave. & 4th NE, Washington, DC 20017; (202) 884-9020; eps.trinitydc.edu. EPS has worked with associations in setting up educational programs, including one on immigration and another on end-of-life issues, approaching each of these topics from the three key sources.

Further Reading

GENERAL DISCUSSION

Davidson, Graeme. *Anyone Can Pray.* Paulist Press, 1983, chapter 7, "Praying with Others," pp. 131–42.
Lumen Gentium (Vatican II).

CONCERNING THEOLOGICAL REFLECTION

Gros, Joye. *Theological Reflection Connecting Faith and Life.* Loyola Press, 2001.

A SHORT LIST OF BOOKS USED FOR DISCUSSION BY SOME EXISTING SMALL FAITH GROUPS

Barry, William A. SJ, and Robert G. Doherty, SJ. *Contemplative in Action*. Paulist Press, 2002.

D'Antonio, William, James Davidson, Dean Hoge, and Mary Gautier. *American Catholics Today*. Rowman & Littlefield, 2007.

DeMello, Anthony, SJ. *Contact with God*. Loyola Press, 1991.

Hellwig, Monika. *Understanding Catholicism*. Paulist Press, 1981.

————. *Public Dimensions of a Believer's Life*. Rowman & Littlefield, 2005.

Magee, Peter. *God's Mercy Revealed*. St. Anthony Messenger Press, 2005.

Massaro, Thomas, SJ. *Living Justice: Catholic Social Teaching in Action*. Rowman & Littlefield, 2000.

Nolan, Albert, OP. *Jesus Before Christianity*. Orbis Books, 1976.

Reiser, William, SJ. *To Hear God's World, Listen to the World*. Paulist Press, 1997.

Underhill, Evelyn. *The School of Charity*. Morehouse Publishing, 1991. (Originally published by Longmans, Green & Co., 1934).

————. *The Spiritual Life*. Morehouse Publishing, 1991. (Originally published by Hodder & Stoughton, 1937).

22

Praying Together with "Prayer Partners"

There has been a long tradition in Catholic homes of the family praying together at the end of the day, either its night prayers or perhaps even the Rosary. This practice is an extension of attending church together as a family. But praying together can also include praying with one's spouse alone, a housebound neighbor, someone sick in the hospital, or even just any friend. Unlike a formal prayer group, praying with someone need not be very carefully scheduled or planned. The most important value is that the two (or three or four) people support one another so that both keep at prayer.

Praying with a friend, family member, or prayer partner can take many forms. In the home, for example, often the busy life of the family leads us to skip praying daily because so many other things demand our attention: by the end of the day we are too tired to pray or forget to do it. We also fight the attraction of television when our favorite shows fill the evening hours. Keeping up a daily commitment to a prayer partner can be a big help to make sure that prayer does not become the rare event in our household.

Prayer with our children is an especially powerful witness to our faith. The proverb that we all learned—"The family that prays together, stays together"—has endured because of its truth. Children grow in faith and prayer through the example and lessons taught by their parents. If parents don't value prayer, how likely is it that the children will as they grow up?

Similarly, when spouses pray together on a regular basis, they can more easily handle the strains and arguments that are sure to come in a marriage. Their respect for the deep life of faith and trust they see in one another will lead them to seek solutions rather than to become more and more suspicious or resentful in disagreements.

Seeking to pray with someone who is homebound or confined to a hospital or nursing home is a great act of Christian mercy. Those who are forced to spend much time alone, and who are suffering or even helpless to take care of themselves, can find friendship and warmth and the sense that someone cares, just from the simple act of having a friend or neighbor stop by to say the Rosary or the Psalms or even our familiar vocal prayers—whether this is each day or a few times a week.

Another possibility for a prayer partner is through correspondence, especially e-mail. Each person shares a prayer or spiritual reading with the other. If they know one another well and like to share thoughts, they can also keep in touch on what their spiritual state is at any given time. There does not have to be a set schedule, although the two people should agree to keep in contact once a week or whatever is suitable for them. There are also a number of religious prayer chat rooms on the Internet that one could join and participate in regularly.

The rules of such prayer are simple: It is a partnership, so each person should be sure that the other is given equal time to be heard. And it is best to agree on a basic format, whether alternately praying aloud, sharing a Scripture passage, praying together in silence, or a combination of all three. The only truly binding rules for such prayer are to keep it comfortable, relaxed, and easy for both of the parties.

23

Retreats

"Come away by yourselves to a deserted place and rest a while."

Mark 6:31

Many of us often experience the desire and need to withdraw from the preoccupations and demands of ordinary daily life. Often it is helpful to make time to get away to a different place to pray or to take a personal inventory of our lives. Making the conscious decision to spend time alone in intense personal prayer in a different location or different kind of physical setting as a way to be renewed in the spiritual life describes the experience of a retreat.

The biblical basis for this way of praying may be found in the Gospels where Jesus, after being baptized by John the Baptist, spent forty days and nights in solitude, praying in the desert (Matt 4:1–2; Mark 1:12–13; Luke 4:1–2). On several occasions during his public ministry of preaching, teaching, and working miracles, Jesus withdrew from others to be alone in prayer (Matt 14:23; Luke 5:16), and he recommended his disciples to do likewise (Mark 6:31). Following the Ascension, the early disciples practiced this advice "to retreat," during which they spent time in seclusion and prayer, awaiting the Holy Spirit to descend upon them at Pentecost (Acts 1:12–14) in order to continue the mission entrusted to them by the resurrected Christ (Luke 24:44–49).

Moving away to a different location characterizes the retreat experience. For example, the desert is a barren and desolate place that does not offer the amenities and conveniences of life. Elijah (1 Kgs 19:4) and John the Baptist (Matt 3:1–5; Luke 3:3–6) spent time alone in the wilderness to encounter God and there came to realize the prophetic mission to which each was being called. Historically, there is a long tradition of monks going into the desert for periods of time to pray, fast, and engage in various forms of penance. The Church Fathers commended this practice. Freed from worldly allures and distractions, one can be drawn closer to God through the experience of solitude.

Removing oneself physically from ordinary daily life so as not to be distracted in prayer is a constitutive component of the retreat experience. Today, retreat houses offer this opportunity at different settings and locations, with specially trained retreat directors who lead spiritual conferences and religious exercises. Many retreat houses advertise on the Internet or in the diocesan newspaper, providing information about upcoming retreats, along with the costs and the available methods of making reservations. It is worthwhile to find a retreat experience that suits your interest and schedule.

Retreats are usually one of two types. The first is called either a *private*, or *directed*, *retreat*, in which a person privately meets with the retreat director at scheduled times. The second type is the *common retreat*, in which a group participates as a whole in conferences, activities, discussions, and spiritual exercises led by a retreat director or retreat team. The daily worship schedule for both kinds of retreat includes Mass, set times for prayer, and opportunities for confession. The length of time for a retreat may be two to three days (often on a weekend), or it may be longer, such as seven to eight days, or even a month. There may be a theme for the retreat, in which there is a schedule of spiritual exercises that retreatants are asked to follow, as well as personal time for silence, prayer, reflection, and leisure.

Religious communities such as the Carmelites, Benedictines, Franciscans, Jesuits, and Passionists have been involved with retreat work for a long time and have trained staffs to assist those desiring to make a retreat. For example, Jesuits offer retreat opportunities based on the classic *Spiritual Exercises* of St. Ignatius Loyola, whereas Carmelites will draw upon the spiritual writings of St. John of the Cross or St. Theresa of Avila.

Unlike a monastic religious order whose members commit themselves to a setting in which regular prayer time and spiritual exercises form the constitutive basis of their daily lives, a retreat offers individuals a short duration away from their ordinary and busy lives to be spiritually renewed and refreshed in a secluded setting. Following the retreat, the person will return to living his or her profession and way of life invigorated by this prayer experience.

Spending time away in prayer during a retreat will allow you to take closer look at your life as well as offers you a way to become more receptive to what God is calling you to do.

24

Pilgrimage as Prayer

From earliest times, the Church has considered pilgrimage to be of great importance. Of course, the Jews of Jesus' day conducted frequent pilgrimages, as witnessed by His own life: When He was a boy, His parents found Him in the Temple after they had "lost him" during their journey to Jerusalem for a religious festival. And the week of Jesus' Passion and death was framed by the pilgrimage of thousands to Jerusalem for the Passover. And so it continued in the Church. Christians came to believe that their souls would benefit from visiting the tombs or other shrines of the martyrs.

As early as the fourth century, men and women from across Europe, Russia, Central Asia, and even Ethiopia flocked to Jerusalem and other sites in the Holy Land. In the subsequent centuries, the faithful undertook pilgrimages to Rome, Santiago de Compostela in Spain, and, later, Canterbury (hence, Chaucer's *Canterbury Tales*). Shrines to Our Lady sprang up at such places as Fatima, Loreto, and Lourdes, and the pilgrims came by the hundreds of thousands, and then the millions.

To speak more specifically about the pilgrimage experience, let's look at Lourdes as an example.

Lourdes: A Pilgrimage Experience

Most Catholics are familiar with at least the outline of the Lourdes story. On February 11, 1858, a fourteen-year-old girl named Bernadette Soubirous looked up from foraging for firewood near the town dump of Lourdes, and saw a lady in white in a niche in the hillside. Bernadette had seventeen subsequent visions and came to know the lady as Mary, the Mother of God. Among the requests that the lady made of her was: "Tell the people to come here in pilgrimage." And so they have, in ever-increasing numbers (more than six million a year at this writing).

The very coming in pilgrimage itself carries a powerful message. As Fr. John Lochran, the longtime chaplain to English-speaking pilgrims in Lourdes, has written:

> The word *pilgrimage* as used by Mary in the local dialect of Bernadette's time means exactly this: to move outside our own secure, familiar place to meet with others. Mary does not just mean pilgrimage as moving from one place to another place. It is above all an invitation to meet not just others but Another. To follow a deeper movement of the spirit, leaving behind our old usual ways of thinking and acting to come to a personal healing encounter with the Lord.

And so the pilgrims come, traveling light (as Jesus told his disciples to do), open to hearing and experiencing something new. They have been willing to leave their comfort zone, exposing themselves to surprises, unfamiliar surroundings, perhaps even disappointments. They do it for themselves to answer the call of Our Lady. They also do it to accompany fellow pilgrims who are poor and sick—to make the pilgrimage possible for them. And they come in a spirit of prayer.

127

Prayer and the Lourdes Pilgrimage

Prayer is woven into nearly every aspect of the Lourdes Pilgrimage. Daily Mass is celebrated in several languages, as is Confession. There are multiple times each day for prayer, including the Rosary, the Stations of the Cross, Eucharistic Adoration, and processions. Each pilgrim also has many opportunities to pray alone. The conditions for prayer are favorable. An air of reverence pervades the atmosphere, especially because most people have made this pilgrimage with faith on their minds. There is plenty of quiet and numerous churches and chapels. No one could doubt that it is an appropriate time and place for reflection.

Often people who have already been to Lourdes return for a different kind of pilgrimage—working for a week to assist the sick who are there for healing. These pilgrims push wheelchairs, help people into and out of the healing water of the shrine's miraculous spring, and perform many other tasks. It is a small surrender of oneself for a week, an acknowledgement of God's grace and our weakness. This is prayer in action.

Further Reading

Cranston, Ruth. *The Miracle of Lourdes*. Image Doubleday, 1988.

Ficocelli, Elizabeth. *Lourdes: Fount of Faith. Hope, and Charity*. Paulist Press, 2009. A unique account that combines a journalist's objectivity and eye for detail with a believer's faith. Includes the author's extraordinary access to the inner workings of the shrine.

Harris, Ruth. *Lourdes: Body and Spirit in the Secular Age*. Viking, 1999. An exploration by a skeptical historian of the events and phenomena of Lourdes, with some surprising conclusions.

Lochran, John. *The Miracle of Lourdes: A Message of Healing and Hope*. St. Anthony Messenger Press, 2008. A marvelous book of meditations on the message of Lourdes by the longtime chaplain to English-speaking pilgrims there.

Martin, James, SJ. *Lourdes Diary: Seven Days at the Grotto of Massabieille*. Loyola, 2006.

Werfel, Franz. *The Song of Bernadette*. Ignatius, 2006. The classic novel, later made into a classic movie.

25

Fasting as Prayer

Fasting is the conscious decision to forego food during a specific period of time for religious reasons. Fasting was known in most ancient societies and throughout most of the world religions. Generally, fasting is done for one of three reasons:

- pleading for God's help in battle or in times of natural disasters
- purifying oneself before a major decision or important event in life
- showing humility and a penitential spirit before God

In times of calamity, people fast to show their dependency on, and faithfulness to, God. Thus, in Jonah 3:7–8, the king of Assyria decrees, "Neither man nor beast, neither cattle nor sheep, shall taste anything; they shall not eat, nor shall they drink water." In the face of a terrible plague of locusts, the prophet Joel cries out, "Proclaim a fast; call an assembly. Gather the elders, all who dwell in the land, into the house of the LORD, your God, and cry to the LORD" (Joel 1:14). Fasting also plays a significant role in the Bible when mourning those who have died (e.g., 1 Sam 31:13).

Examples of purifying oneself can be seen in the three-day fast of St. Paul as he waited to find out God's will after being struck down on the road to Damascus (Acts 9:9). Jesus himself prepared for his public ministry by a forty-day fast (Mark 1:12–13). The Catholic Church has traditionally celebrated days of fasting on the vigil before major feasts such as Christmas, Easter, and Pentecost. Ember days and Rogation days were established to mark both the liturgical seasons and the natural change of seasons each quarter of the year.

The practice of fasting out of humility and penance is also a long tradition in the Church. For example, in the moving scene when Ezra calls on the people to accept the Torah, "the Israelites gathered together fasting and in sackcloth, their heads covered with dust...then they stood forth and confessed their sins and the guilty deeds of their fathers" (Neh 9:1–2). The Psalms often speak of fasting: "I humbled myself with fasting" (Ps 69:11); "I afflicted myself with fasting and poured forth prayers within my bosom" (Ps 35:13). Israelite Law required only one solemn fast a year, the Day of Atonement, but in general, fasting was an important part of Old Testament faith. However, it must be from the heart. Isaiah 58:4–7 warns us against the false spirit of fasting—and advises us to take on the true:

> Yes, your fasting ends in quarreling and fighting,
>   striking with wicked claw;
> Would that today you might fast
>   so as to make your voice heard on high!
> Is this the manner of fasting I wish,
>   of keeping a day of penance:
> that one bows his head like a reed,
>   and lie in sackcloth and ashes?

Do you call this day a fast,
  a day acceptable to the LORD?

This rather is the fasting that I wish:
  releasing those bound unjustly,
  untying the thongs of the yoke,
setting free the oppressed,
  breaking every yoke;
sharing your bread with the hungry,
  sheltering the oppressed and the homeless,
clothing the naked when you see them,
and not turning your back on your own.

The Church has always encouraged fasting to deepen our awareness of our dependence on God rather than on material goods. The practice of fasting all day on Wednesdays and Fridays was common in the early Church: no food or drink was taken from dawn until dusk. About AD 400, the Church substituted Saturday instead as the special day of penance and fasting; in modern times, Friday was made the day of fasting. It allowed for small amounts of food but the total amount should add up to no more than one solid meal, and no meat was allowed. Monastic communities and others often kept more rigorous practices of fasting. Although fasting on Fridays outside of Lent is no longer an obligation, it is strongly encouraged by the Church.

The values of fasting are thus many. All Catholics should find ways to incorporate fasting into their prayer life. It allows us to combine our prayer of obedience to God with our confession of sinfulness, and it reminds us at the same time that what we have in abundance must be shared with those who have less. All days of fasting should be carried out in a quiet and unassuming way, recalling Jesus' own command to us: "When you fast, do not look gloomy like the hypocrites who neglect their appearance so that they may appear to others as fasting...but when you fast, anoint your head and wash your face so that you may not appear to be fasting, except to your Father who is hidden" (Matt 6:16–18).

Jesus also suggested that we fast as a sign of our awareness that we still await his Second Coming. He tells the Pharisees and scribes who complain that his disciples do not fast, "Can the wedding guests fast while the bridegroom is with them?...But the time will come when the bridegroom will be taken from them, and on that day they will fast" (Mark 2:19–20).

A decision to fast does not have to pertain to giving up food or drink. We can choose to deny ourselves other enjoyments or addictions that we have, or to deprive ourselves of an hour of sleep; for example, to pray or to do some work of justice or charity. If it does involve food, however, it does not have to be a total fast. Giving up one meal a day, having a simpler meal for dinner, allowing liquids but not solid foods during the day, or not eating during the day until after sunset (as the Muslims and Jews do), are all traditional possibilities. In general, however, it would be most meaningful for most people to try to observe some sort of fasting or abstinence on Fridays, as the Church encourages each of us to commit ourselves to join in prayer and witness with the universal community of God's people. Such a day of fasting, whether strict or only partial, should also include a special resolution to pray with a twofold purpose: to praise God for his goodness and acknowledge our dependence on Him, and to seek forgiveness for our faults in a true spirit of penance.

26

Using Icons and Art for Prayer

Praying before an image of Christ, the Blessed Virgin Mary, or one of the saints is a time-honored tradition for Western Catholics and Eastern Christians alike. Most of our religious art in the West is representational and lifelike, not abstract, and so we are often stirred by the expression on the face of the figure. We are also moved by the emotional depiction of a tragic scene, such as Christ's last agony, Mary's tenderness holding her child, or a saint's dramatic martyrdom. Churches in both Europe and the United States are filled with art by both well-known and little-known artists to help us pray by its lifelike imagery. It is customary for Catholics to offer a prayer before the images that are found on side altars or walls of a church, perhaps even to light a candle before the painting or statue so that the prayer will be "continued" even when we have left the church to go home. This practice is recognized by the Church as a help to prayer: praying before an image in church unites us to the communion of the Blessed Virgin and the saints who surround the throne of God in heaven.

The use of the Eastern Church's tradition of icons is slightly different. An icon is not intended to be a highly realistic painting or one filled with emotional impact. It is painted to lack the roundedness of real figures and without the perspective of depth, in order to keep it from being an image or likeness of God, as forbidden by the first commandment in Exodus 20. There are also strict rules that, of the Trinity, only Christ may be rendered in full human form, but never God the Father or the Holy Spirit, because Christ was the incarnate and risen savior among us.

Despite these constraints, an icon is a portrait of a person or persons, with much attention on the face. Although icons often seem fixed and wooden as they stare out at the believer, each is intended to invite us into the mystery behind the face or scene and to find the presence of God there. We are not asked to feel the emotion of the moment, but to become aware of the divine grace that worked in the person or scene that is painted. For this reason, the eyes in an icon are often larger than usual so that we can see into the soul behind the surface of the painting.

Indeed, Eastern Christians often speak of the icon as not painted at all, but written. Each unlocks the Divine Word of God's revelation through that saint or biblical scene. The one who prays with the icon then "reads" its different symbols and traditional elements. The depictions are rarely completely original, but follow the traditional ways that Mary or John the Baptist or others have been drawn from ages past. And yet each icon is also the unique work of an inspired painter, so that no two are ever exactly alike. Icons of the Greek Church tend to be sharper and bolder, while those of the Russian Church tradition use more curves and softer lines. But in all of them, the major qualities seem to be balance, harmony, and peace. We can often see two other qualities that alternate depending on the subject matter: ascetical strength or tenderness. No matter which, the positioned figures and the surrounding space create a silence and mystery that invites us to contemplative prayer.

In praying with an icon, it is important to set it up so it stands by itself and you can look on its shape and configuration. Ask what it represents, what mystery it invites us to contemplate, what its most important symbolic images are. Famous icons—like the portrait of Our Lady of Perpetual Help who is holding Jesus for us to see, or Andrei Rublev's depiction of the three angels who visited Abraham—have elaborate symbols that take us away from an emotional response to order to proclaim the truths of faith in the Incarnation and the Trinity. In each case, we look beyond the feeling the icon creates and ask what its implication is for our lives.

Ann Persson, in her book *The Circle of Love: Praying with Rublev's Icon of the Trinity*, quotes the great English mystic Julian of Norwich as providing us the ideal prayer before the icon:

> We are enfolded in the Father and we are enfolded in the Son and we are enfolded in the Holy Spirit. And the Father is enfolded in us and the Son is enfolded in us and the Holy Spirit is enfolded in us....Our soul rests in God, its true peace; our soul stands in God, its true strength, and is deep rooted in God for endless love.

Further Reading

Forrest, Jim. *Praying with Icons*. Orbis, 2008.

Nouwen, Henri. *Behold the Beauty of the Lord*. Ave Maria Press, 2007.

Persson, Ann. *The Circle of Love: Praying with Rublev's icon of the Trinity*. Bible Reading Fellowship, 2010.

Williams, Rowan. *The Dwelling of the Light: Praying with Icons of Christ*, Eerdmans, 2003.

27

Poetry and Songs

> Let the word of Christ dwell in you richly...
> singing psalms, hymns, and spiritual songs with
> gratitude in your hearts to God.
>
> Colossians 3:16

How often do lyrics from a song or words from a poem keep recurring in our mind? While a great deal of communication is frequently done in ordinary conversation and written prose, the language of poetry and music offer a different form for artistic expression. Poems and songs seem to flow more from the heart rather than the mind.

Whereas prose is straightforward and sequential, fostering a cognitive sense of understanding, poetry and music use words differently in imaginative and creative ways. Poems and songs come alive in way that involves the auditory sense of attentively listening to the words, as well as the interior act of reflecting upon the meaning of them. Poems and songs are meant to be heard aloud, not read quietly.

Poems and songs are repeated time and time again. What is expressed in verses and lyrics tends to arise more from the inner workings of the human spirit. Unlike prose that is clear-cut and informational, poetry and music have an abstract, elusive, symbolic, and hidden meaning, as well as a mysterious sense that prompts further reflection beyond the superficial level of simply listening to the words.

The 150 Psalms found in the Bible were originally composed as religious songs to be sung or as poetic expressions to be recited in prayer. For this reason, the responsorial Psalms are often sung in the Liturgy of the Word at Mass. In this form of prayer, the words and phrases from the Psalms evoke images and thoughts about God and God's relationship with humanity, such as "The LORD is my shepherd" (Ps 23:1), "The LORD is my rock, my fortress, my deliverer (Ps 18:2), "I wait for you, O LORD, I lift up my soul (Ps 25:1), and "Have mercy on me, God" (Ps 51:3). Consider listening attentively to both the words of the Psalm as well as the response that you are singing. You may even find yourself singing these words apart from the liturgy that you are attending.

"The person who sings, prays twice"—a popular quote attributed to St. Augustine—reminds us how music, hymns, and songs are ways to pray. Sacred music, hymns, and songs have a long tradition of conveying themes and images for prayer.

In addition to compositions that are set to music, poems have expressed images and thoughts that can be used to meditate and pray. The works of such renowned poets as Gerard Manley Hopkins, T. S. Eliot, G. K. Chesterton, Joyce Kilmer, John Henry Newman, and others, illustrate how this artistic writing form has been utilized to convey religious thoughts and spiritual insights. Poetry offers a way to be a teaching device in which the repetition of a phrase, thought, or key word remains with the listener after the poem has been read.

While already-written poetry and songs are opportunities for prayer and reflection, many us have an inner artistic ability and a yearning to compose our own poetic verses and lyrics. Instead of carefully written prose, poems and songs allow a more free-form way to express ourselves. You may consider creative ways to express your innermost thoughts, feelings, and thoughts in a prayer to God similar to what the Psalmist did. In this artistic form of expression, there is no one right way or wrong way to compose words that flow from your heart. These are *your* words and *your* way of praying.

Even poems and songs that come from a nonreligious or even a secular setting may offer the possibilities for praying, since poetry and music are frequently used as a means to express human experience. We may identify with what the poet or composer is conveying since it resonates with our own lives. These words or images can be used in a way of praying that is open-ended and free-flowing like verses and lyrics, and differs from formal types of praying that follow the exact and precise wording of prose.

As St. John Damascene noted: "Prayer is the raising of one's mind and heart to God" (*Catechism of the Catholic Church* #2559). Since prayer is an activity that involves the mind and heart, the popular image of using both the right and left side of the brain, balancing the logical and the creative sides of ourselves, should also apply to praying.

Poetry and songs offer creative and imaginative ways from our innermost being (our hearts) to express our deepest longings, thoughts, and desires (our minds) that may be brought before God in prayer.

28

Media Prayer

> The information provided by the media is at the service of the common good. Society has a right to information based on truth, freedom, justice, and solidarity.
>
> *Catechism of the Catholic Church #2494*

Advances in technology enable instantaneous mass communication of information that is accessible in many different media. Indeed, news does travel quickly: television, radio, cell phones, iPhones, BlackBerries, text messaging, and the Internet provide ways for the worldwide community to keep immediately informed and aware about what is occurring up to the very minute that news is being reported. The latest natural disaster, an act of terrorism or violence, the results of international meetings, the death of a significant individual or celebrity, a drastic change in the stock market, the pope's latest message, and so on: the news about each spreads very quickly. Media disseminates information widely, shaping societal attitudes as well as influencing human behavior and actions.

Karl Barth, a significant twentieth-century Swiss theologian, recommended a "two-handed" approach in the Christian daily life, reportedly saying that one "should carry the Bible in one hand and the daily newspaper in the other." The Second Vatican Council's *Gaudium et Spes*, the Pastoral Constitution on the Church in the Modern World (1965), as well as subsequent postconciliar teaching, reiterates that the "Church exists in, not apart from, the modern world." Believers need to be informed and involved about daily events locally, nationally, and internationally. By becoming aware of events reported in the media, these can become opportunities for prayer.

Immediate news of natural disasters often prompts a generous response and an outpouring of donations when we see others afflicted. These images may also become a means for us to pray for those who have been adversely affected, as well as for the success of assistance and relief missions. Political meetings in which important issues and topics are being deliberated may encourage us to pray for wisdom and divine guidance for those who hold public office. Terrorism, violence, and injustice recall the Gospel challenge to "love your enemies and pray for those who persecute you" (Matt 5:43). The successful rescue mission in which a human life has been saved, act of heroism, or the significant achievement of a person or group who has been recognized as doing well may prompt a prayer of gratitude to God.

While viewing television or using the various modes of electronic communication may be seen as a passive activity, how we respond to the information that we receive can prompt us to be more attentive as well as challenge us to act. We become better informed as Christians of the pressing issues of the day, mindful that the Church exists in this modern society. Media can serve as the catalyst for thought, reflection, and prayer. The images that we view and the information that we learn call forth a personal response.

A television documentary about environmental issues may make us more aware of the world as God's gift to humanity and encourage a prayerful response as to how we are stewards of God's creation. Listening to the radio, reading the newspaper, obtaining information from the Internet are effective ways to become cognizant that we do not live alone as isolated individuals. St. Paul's image of the Body of Christ is a helpful social analogy that reminds us, "God has so constructed the body...that there may be no division in the body, but that the parts may have the same concern for one another. If (one) part suffers, all the parts suffer with it; if one part is honored, all the parts share its joy"(1 Cor 12:24-26).

Based upon we what have seen, heard, or read, both the "good" and the "bad" news communicated via the media offer two important ways to pray:

1. *Thanksgiving*—prayers of gratitude in which we give thanks to God
2. *Intercessory*—prayers in which we ask for God's guidance and help in daily life along with praying for the needs of others and the world